SAMUEL

CHADWICK

Preacher and Evangelist

Herbert Boyd McGonigle

MA, BD, DD, PHD

Former Lecturer at Nazarene Theological College, Dene Road, Didsbury, Manchester, in the classes in Church History, Theology and Wesley Studies, Former Principal of Nazarene Theological College and now Principal Emeritus

British Library Cataloguing in Publication Data.
A catalogue record for this book is available from the British Library

ISBN 978 0 86071 737 9

A Commissioned Publication Printed by
MOORLEYS
Print, Design & Publishing
info@moorleys.co.uk · www.moorleys.co.uk

I met the Revd. Paul James, MA, the first time that Jeanne and I attended Southport in 1977. His father, the Revd. Maynard James, told me that one of his three sons was Vicar in the Church of England and we both met Paul. He was a regular contributor to the Flame, and attending Southport we came to know one another. When I came to write, Samuel Chadwick: Preacher and Evangelist, *I thought of him. Many a time Maynard James told me about Samuel Chadwick and said that he was raised up to form Cliff College. Paul and I got on well and he has made a number of trips to the Nazarene Theological College, Manchester. As both of us have retired, I wish him well and pray that the Lord will make us willing and obedient in the day of His power.*

FOREWORD

I felt very honoured when Dr. Herbert McGonigle asked me to write this Foreword to his new book, 'Samuel Chadwick, Preacher and Evangelist.' I have known Herbert as a friend and adviser for many years and he was very supportive when I wrote a biography of my own father, Maynard James.

Samuel Chadwick was a household name in my parents' home and my father often talked of the influence that he had on his life. Maynard went up to Cliff College in January 1927, having been a lay preacher in the Cardiff Holiness Mission. Chadwick immediately took an interest in him and soon made him student leader, asking him to stay on for two extra terms. Under Chadwick's direction Maynard was a leader on one of the famous Cliff College treks, which was greatly blessed and became a pattern for treks and evangelistic outreach of both the International Holiness Mission and the Calvary Holiness Church. My father's first pastorate at the Manchester Tabernacle was partly due to Chadwick's support.

But Herbert's book has given me a much clearer picture of Chadwick. I never met him, unless it was as a babe in arms, as he died after I was born. I didn't realise that he was brought up in Burnley where I lived as a boy and the book has brought back many memories. For example, the sound of clogs as workers passed the bedroom in the early hours on the way to the mill. The deafening noise of the looms, where I was taken by a family friend who worked in one of the factories. And to think that Chadwick worked in one of these when he was under ten years of age! Herbert has brought to life those years of toil and study which led Samuel Chadwick eventually to become a very able scholar and Bible expositor. But most of all the book reveals what an outstanding man of God he was. Prayer was at the heart of it and a life filled by the Holy Spirit. He became a leading Methodist preacher, teacher, Principal, and Chairman of Conference. Sometimes the great teaching of Holiness and entire Sanctification, which John and Charles Wesley emphasised so strongly, is put to one side or even denied, but Chadwick had it at the forefront of his ministry.

The book, along with other of Herbert's recent books, is to be commended for its insights. It is remarkable that Herbert has gone forward after major illness and also the illness and death of his beloved Jeanne. I pray for God's blessing on this book, which I hope will be widely read, including being read throughout the Methodist Church of which Samuel Chadwick was a towering figure.

Revd. Paul James MA
Church Stretton
Shropshire
June 2017

Samuel Chadwick

Preacher and Evangelist

Samuel Chadwick was born at No. 8, Baldwin Street, Burnley, Lancashire, on September 16, 1860, the oldest of six children. His father and mother were members of Wesley Chapel, Hargreaves Street, Burnley, holding about fifteen hundred people. While Samuel was yet a child, he was moved to No. 6, Back Hammerton Street, where he was brought up. Writing of his experience forty years later, Samuel commented:

> It would be difficult to imagine anything more drab, prosaic, and uninteresting than our street. Its name was its only distinction, for it was named after the only distinguished man of letters Burnley has produced. There was not a blade of grass, a tree, or a flower in our area. It hummed with the noise of factories from morning until night. The only playground was the kerb stone, and when you were not in the living-room you were in the bedroom. Not much of a place to be brought up in, but there was some good bringing-up done in that drab area of cottages.[1]

Grandfather Chadwick led the prayer-meetings in Wesley Chapel at seven o'clock and later on Samuel was told that Grandfather Chadwick had a great gift in prayer, that he was one of seven brothers who were all soldiers and that he got converted under one of Wesley's preachers. His father and mother met in Sunday School and all their children were baptised in the chapel and Samuel was taken to Sunday School before he could walk. When he was just eight, his father took him to the mill and used him to labour there among his fellows. The mill in which he worked belonged to Methodists and he never heard a curse or swearing. While still in his eighth year, he signed the Temperance Pledge, for he saw drunkenness in his earliest years for there were drunkards in three of the five houses in Back Hammerton Street. The

---

1 Norman Dunning, *Samuel Chadwick*, p.27.

boy grew to be a man and there was born within him a deadly and fiery hatred of drink. When still a youth, he turned up at a meeting on the Band of Hope Committee and opposed the election of the Superintendent Minister as President because he had seen a barrel of beer carried from the cart through the front door of the manse.

From the age of eight till he was twenty-one, he worked in the mill and his meagre offerings were handed to his mother. The Chadwicks were not well off and it took the wages of father and son to help the family. For the fifteen years he had worked with his father, his wage helped out his mother and for the years left to his father, he kept up a part of his earnings and sent them to his father. Norman Dunning, in his 'Prologue' to his book, tells of a story known only to Samuel and himself.

> How he loved his own folks! His devotion to them, even to the end of his life, was more than touching. One of the last things I did for him was to run down to the village post-office and register a letter to a chosen among his loved ones. Sickness had fallen upon the home, and he was sending a few pound notes. When his father was beginning to fail, the eldest son was at hand to help. 'Father, don't go to the mill any more, and I will pay you your wages every week.' For twenty-two years, out of his stipend as a minister, he kept his father's home.[2]

Samuel was converted at the age of ten and the preacher was the Revd. Samuel Coley, who taught theology at Headingly College, Leeds, for the training of Wesleyan ministers. The preacher read the first Psalm and he spoke on, 'A Lily among Thorns', and he arrested the boy when he talked about John Newton, who had said that if he were a shoe-black, he would be the best shiner of shoes in his village. When the preacher talked about shining boots the boy sat up.

> It was a simple thing to do, but I believe, in the light of after years, that it was the most important thing I ever did in my life. It was the adoption of a fixed principle from which I have never gone back. I got into the habit of doing the simplest duties as unto, and for, Jesus Christ. I have written thousands of letters a year, but I do not know that I have sent one with a blot on it, or with a word crossed out.... I went apart three times

---

[2] Norman Dunning, *Samuel Chadwick*, p.22.

> a day and prayed in spirit all the time between. The habit of three times a day was not easy. The dinner hour was short, the family was large, and the house small, but I managed.[3]

Five years later he joined a Society Class whose leader was Ambrose Broughton, a man of refined taste and spiritual nature. At fifteen the awakening mind was definitely called to the ministry. He had practically no education and his people were poor but he gave proof of his call by becoming a serious and strenuous student. He was at work from six in the morning until six at night but by seven o'clock he was at his books and for five hours struggling over grammar and arithmetic, geography and history, theology and the Bible.

When Samuel was sixteen Josiah Mee discovered his secret and from then on, he found a life-long friend. Within weeks he began to preach and in order to have a sitting room in which to study, the family moved from Back Hammerton Street to a house in Junction Street which had a parlour. Josiah Mee was succeeded by Dr. Waddy Moss in the Burnley Circuit and a new influence came into the life of the young preacher. Dr. Moss was a prodigy in learning and a master of exposition. Samuel used to say that if he had to choose one preacher whose ministry he must sit Sunday by Sunday, Waddy Moss would be his choice. When he came before the Local Preacher's Meeting, the whole gathering gave him a hearty and unanimous vote. Afterwards Waddy Moss spoke to him in the vestry and passed on the name of his successor. Encouraged by one Superintendent to offer himself as a candidate, Chadwick was immediately discouraged by the Revd. William Ford, the man's successor, who made a point of never offering a candidate who had no culture or education. The way ahead seemed closed to the young preacher and it led him, in subsequent years, to champion those on grounds of education, believing that the call of God the most essential qualification. Josiah Mee had moved to the Bacup Circuit and Samuel Chadwick, already having a considerable local reputation as a preacher, was invited to become a lay evangelist at Stacksteads.

---

[3] Norman Dunning, *Samuel Chadwick*, pp.30, 31.

Stacksteads was fifteen miles from Burnley and it boasted a population of 6000 people, twelve public houses, one parish church and four nonconformist places of worship. The Methodist Church staff felt a special mission lasting two or three weeks wasn't long enough and that Stacksteads needed an evangelist of its own. The Revd. Josiah Mee thought about Samuel Chadwick and they talked and prayed and promised to give him 18/6 per week. Chadwick arrived from Burnley and the next day began 'my first adventure of Faith and Love.' He had fifteen sermons all prepared and he had preached a dozen of them, yet the revival had not come. The two years he spent in Stacksteads determined the direction of his life. The large new chapel and Sunday School was there but small congregations posed problems. Chadwick always had a desire to be a preacher but the more time he spent in Stacksteads finally won him over to be an evangelist. Britain was full of preachers but there was a scarceness of evangelists. For the twenty-one old evangelist the whole situation changed as his interest was aroused in the doctrine of scriptural holiness. He had been reading sermons by the Revd. J. Denholm Brash on the subject and when he looked in to his sermons, there seemed to be a lack of power and presence.

> It was Saturday night and his thoughts were on the morrow. He was going over his notes for the last time. God put his finger on the sermons and the young preacher understood. He had believed his strength was in the sermons, and had forgotten that God alone is able to save. There was s struggle. It went on through the midnight hour. At three o'clock on the Sunday morning a fire was kindled in the kitchen grate and the sermons were burned. The blessing had come. The work of converting began that day. At the early morning prayer-meeting he witnessed to an experience of sanctification, and led his first convert to Jesus. Before the day closed seven people were converted. As he used to say, God gave him one for every barren year of his preaching.[4]

The revival started and every community in the town was shaken. One night there came to a meeting the most notorious drunkard in the town. His name was Robert Hamer but everyone knew him as 'Bury Bob.' He had been guilty of every crime in the calendar except murder. He

---

4 Norman Dunning, *Samuel Chadwick*, p.43.

had fought a fierce bulldog with his hands tied behind his back, killed rats with his teeth, eaten glass, smashed furniture, wrecked public bars, mauled policemen and fought all-comers. His presence in a religious meeting was a sensation. When he walked to a table and asked for a pledge card the excitement was overwhelming. He took the pen and made a cross opposite his name. The following he was glorious saved. Next morning he was first at the quarry and he told them what had happened. On the steps Samuel Chadwick announced that Bob would testify to the grace that saved him in the evening service. On Sunday night the chapel was full to hear what Jesus had done to raise the dead. The revival went on for months and hundreds of the very worst were glorious saved.

The work under Samuel Chadwick grew and his sermons filled the chapel. He was determined to candidate for the ministry and Church and a Church of England clergyman was his Greek tutor; he read all his books with serious intention. Every afternoon he visited, getting to know the people who came to his church. It appears from his Journal that his father and mother were in indifferent health and his devotion to his home folks was so great that it lasted him throughout his days. At the end of the year in Stacksteads the chance for him came and it is to the lasting ministry of Bacup Church that his chance came. But it was not to be. The opposition in the July Committee was strong and they delayed his coming for a year. He was disappointed but his heart was set. He went back to Stacksteads and he toiled and prayed and visited his people. The blessing of heaven attended his ministry and next July he applied and was accepted.

Samuel attended the Didsbury College, Manchester, from 1883 to 1886. Didsbury was established in 1842 and by the time that Samuel attended, the College was growing fast. He was a student for three years and he attended every lecture and all classes. At first the lectures were difficult but he stayed with the work and was helped by friends and teachers who found the young man easy to get on with. At Didsbury Chadwick was taught by the Revd. William Burt Pope, with whom he studied assiduously and Dr. Pope's main work, *Compendium of Christian Theology*, was always in his hand. He met three friends who were to prove lifelong companions; Herbert Workman, who later became Principal of Westminster Wesleyan Training College, Frederick Luke Wiseman who became Connexional Home Mission Evangelist, and Edward Davidson who became a Connexional Evangelist. Luke Wiseman in particular shared Mission Anniversary and Cliff College platforms with Chadwick and, as Connexional Home Mission secretary, was responsible for Chadwick's appointment as Principal of Cliff College in 1912. The final act of that friendship was in delivering the address at Chadwick's funeral on October 20, 1932.

Samuel Chadwick as a student at Didsbury College

As a first year preacher, Samuel Chadwick was given the honour of preaching at the week-night in St. Paul, Didsbury. At that period St. Paul's was one of the best-known churches in English Methodism. Originally built as a Church of England, the Bishop of Manchester turned it down and it was offered to the Methodists. The young preacher was not overawed by the fact that he was preaching to his fellow students and to the Principal and Tutors. At a point in the sermon he began to tell the people of a Church where there had been a revival and how the people came forward to seek the Saviour. He described the scene at the penitent-form and looked round at the beautiful architecture of the church. As Norman Dunning explains:

> Then with a sweep of his arm, he said, 'Oh, it was not a Church like this. It was a Church that was built for the purpose of getting people converted.' The Staff did not like the sermon. Dr. Workman wrote: 'I shall never forget his sermon to us, as a first-rate man in the College Chapel, and in which all his great qualities were revealed. Later in the week I was taking supper with the Governor, the Revd. William Jackson, who I learned was not favourably disposed towards the preacher. I ventured to differ from the Governor, and to say in my humble judgement Chadwick would become one of the great forces in our Churches, and if he lived, would certainly become a President.' The following day, when the Governor, Dr. Jackson, read out the plan of appointments for the week-end, he concluded by saying, 'And if any of you men this week-end happen to come across the ugliest Church in Methodism, let me know, and we'll send Mr. Chadwick there to preach.'[5]

During his first year in college, Samuel met Thomas Cook, who was conducting a mission somewhere in the neighbourhood of Manchester. He had come to Didsbury to see his friend Edward Davison and the three of them had a prayer-meeting in Chadwick's lodging. Chadwick never forgot that hour. He saw the glory of God in the faces of these men. He felt the power of their prayers and on the following Sunday, when they went out to preach, all three had a wonderful harvest. A few days later he went to hear Thomas Cook preach and his sermon puzzled Chadwick. When the appeal was made, hundreds went to the enquiry room. The preacher looked like a mere boy and the sermon was not mature, but in the after-meeting, the youth was a master of assemblies.

The origin of the first Southport Methodist Holiness Convention, held in 1885, led to Samuel Chadwick and his friend, Thomas Cook, the first Connexional Evangelist in the Wesleyan Methodist Church, being

---

[5] Norman Dunning, *Samuel Chadwick*, p.61.

the first people to be asked. Already there were stirrings within the Wesleyan Church, as well as other branches of Methodism and these encouraged the pioneers of Southport. In 1871, four young Wesleyan ministers co-operated to spread the biblical doctrine of entire sanctification as taught by the Wesleys. Several tracts were published and in the year 1872, a magazine, entitled, *The King's Highway*, was launched, with Revd. Isaac Page as editor. From the same year on, meetings for the promotion of holiness were held during the Wesleyan Conference. In 1874 a similar gathering took place in Wakefield at West Parade Chapel. These were the harbingers of the Southport Convention to be launched in June 1885.

> In the spring of that year Thomas Cook led a most fruitful mission at Trinity, Southport, at the invitation of William Tindall. It was during the course of this campaign that these two men were brought together to the conviction that they must call a Convention for the purpose of spreading Scriptural holiness throughout the land according to John Wesley's own vision. It is significant that they invited two young students in training for the ministry at Didsbury College, Manchester, to share in the running of the project – Samuel Chadwick, future Principal of Cliff College after Cook, and Edward Davidson, who had worked with Cook as an evangelist and later became a Connexional Evangelist. Plans were made to hold five days of meetings from Monday, 22nd June, 1885. Samuel Chadwick was appointed as President in 1914.[6]

In this way Chadwick joined the first Methodist Convention in Southport in 1885 and was elected in 1914 appointed as President of the Convention. He remain as President until his death while John Broadbelt was elected as President. Many fine people have been elected to this office but no one has surpassed Samuel Chadwick in the power and presence he exerted over the Southport Convention.

In the summer of 1886, the College course was over, and the following September Chadwick entered upon the first year of probation in Nicholson Square Circuit, Edinburgh. The Scottish capital made a great impression upon him. It was a city of preachers. Dr. Alexander White was at Free St. George's Church and it was a place that was

---

6 A. Skevington Wood, *Let Us Go On*, 1985, pp.9, 10, 21.

usually crowded with listeners. Henry Drummond was at the zenith of his powers in the University. John McNeil was sweeping Edinburgh and many crowded to listen. Dr. Matheson, the blind preacher, was preaching regularly at St. Bernard's, while Dr. Smith was at Free High Church. At Albany Street Congregational Chapel, Dr. John Pulsford preached to a full church, and Dr. Landels was drawing crowds to Dublin Street Baptist Church. The young Methodist probationer revelled in his opportunity as he listened to these pulpit giants. He talked to men who wrote books and in this university city felt the stimulus of ripe scholarship and intellectual greatness. His Superintendent was the Revd. John Martin, the Chairman of the Scotland District. Together they held missions in all their preaching places and Chadwick grew to love the Scottish people. Thirty years later, when he was Principal of Cliff College, Samuel counted it a privilege to be asked again to Edinburgh and to conduct a mission in that city.

Chadwick wrote of this experience thirty-two years later.

> Edinburgh was in God's plan. Often as a missionary I was glad to remember those wonderful days. When superior people said how suitable I was for mission-work and very plainly implied it was not up to their standard, I said to myself: 'Anyhow, I have been to Edinburgh!' The social life of the city was stimulating, and its air of culture I have never forgotten, but its work of Evangelism and the pastoral care of its young people possessed me. Great changes have taken place in thirty-two years. A generation has practically gone. Instead of the fathers are the children. The young people of those days have grown-up sons and daughters of their own. The fruit abides. I meet them all over the country, and nothing has borne better fruit than my Society Class of boys from about ten to fifteen years of age.[7]

Chadwick served his time in Edinburgh and used that discipline in a strict study and spent it in tackling solid books as well as developing a Scottish style of exegetical preaching.

---

7 D.W. Lambert, *The Testament of Samuel Chadwick 1860-1932*, p.19.

The years 1887-1890 were spent in Glasgow and he moved into a new church at Clydebank. Chadwick was the first minister to serve the new church and it opened after serving eighteen months in a local public hall. His ministry included open-air preaching, temperance rallies and 'men only' meetings including question and answer sessions. Originally the people did not know him and they found him preaching the gospel near his church building. He found a place where there was a row of houses, a chair was provided and the young man stood there without a word. People gathered and presently there was a crowd. The preacher remained silent and people shouted, 'He's selling pills,' and, 'What is it for Governor?' The crowd was excited and then Chadwick spoke. It was his first sermon to the audience in Clydebank. Within a few days the whole town was talking about him and the church filled up and he started at the beginning. In a letter to a friend, he explained how poor he was and that his father had subscribed more for a theological training at Didsbury and in those years of probation he paid back every penny. Norman Dunning explains how drink was his major foe and he fought it with all his might.

> The Brewers had secured the most strategic positions for the public houses, and application were in for five new licenses. I found that as a minister I had some standing in the court, and resolved to take my courage in both hands and do what I could. The barrister who held the brief for the brewers made sport of my calling, and wound up his banter with the withering sarcasm: 'I should like to ask this young-looking shepherd, what hast thou done with the sheep in the wilderness?' Quick as thought I sprang to my feet and flung out the answer, 'Don't you trouble about my sheep, I am after the wolf to-day.'[8]

A Memorial Church had been built in the new industrial centre and Chadwick had been appointed there. He began by preaching out of doors and at most of the services whiskey bottles went down the gutter-grates. The pub owners were upset at Chadwick's preaching and drunken men were sent to upset the meetings but all was in vain. Conversions began the first Sunday and continued until drunkards were converted and joined the church. Looking back on those

---

[8] D.W. Lambert, *The Testament of Samuel Chadwick*, p.67.

Clydebank days, Samuel spoke of those months as being Spirit-filled and armed with God's protection.

> I preached twice every Sunday and gave Bible lectures in the afternoon to a Church crowded with men. We ranted like Salvationists and studied like divinity students. Miracles of grace abounded. Drunkards were delivered, and we fought the drink with a perfect fury of enthusiasm. Those were great and wonderful days, in spite of much physical weakness and many adventures.... I am glad God made me an Evangelist. There is no reward in affection and devotion like that which comes to the winner of souls.[9]

For three years the revival continued at Clydebank and the name of the young minister was becoming known in Methodism and in 1890, when he was ordained, his new appointment was discussed in Conference. Thomas Champness caused a sensation by proposing that Samuel Chadwick should be sent as Superintendent of the Leeds Mission. John Shaw Banks, the Superintendent of the District, strongly supported the proposal and the Conference agreed. Banks had made the acquaintance of Chadwick during a ten days' mission at Chapel Allerton and the young preacher had been released from his Church in Glasgow.

On his way north after Ordination, the newly-appointed Superintendent visited the place he was to serve and he was told by the steward that they had tamed bigger men and were not ashamed. Chadwick tells the story as one who was present and he leaves nothing out. The stewards who had come to the station did not know him and passed him on the platform. He arrived at the Superintendent's house with his sister, who was to be his housekeeper and a maid she had brought with her. The stewards came in as Samuel had finished tea and the banter soon took over; the stewards were not happy that they had not invited him. They were in debt and they could not be responsible for financing the Mission. They complained that they could not be responsible and a reduction in finance was proposed seeing their young minister was not married. Samuel listened to their proposal and pointed

---

9 Samuel Chadwick, *The Testament of Samuel Chadwick*, p.20.

out that he had not come to them now that he was a Superintendent and he had never asked for a rise. Eventually Samuel said that he would take all financial responsibility and proposed a rise though he was not sure where the money was coming from. In less than six months a heavy debt was removed and the rise was given unasked. He went to visit 'the Midden,' where every afternoon two or three thousand gamblers met in open-air gambling exchange. It went in the first six months and Samuel was rejoicing, not in one Lazarus but in half a dozen. The revival began on the first Sunday and by the end of September the Chapel was full half an hour before the time to begin and police regulated the crowd. The Wesley Church in Leeds was Samuel's growing ministry and the people were the saintliest that he had ever known. Chadwick was there three years and the Church was packed every Sunday morning and evening.

One of Chadwick's greatest helpers was Tommy Doughill. He was a cobbler and was bow-legged. Tommy was converted under Chadwick's preaching and began to preach and was known as quite a character in the neighbourhood. He called at a house one day to collect a pair of shoes, and the lady introduced him to the curate who was paying a pastoral visit. The curate was amazed at the information that this illiterate cobbler was a preacher and especially when Tommy preceded to give him an outline he had preached a week before. His subject was 'Three Fools,' and the first point was that he was a fool for not believing that there is no God in the realm of his thinking. The second fool was the man who said, 'Eat, drink and be merry,' for he was a fool in the realm of his living. The third fool was a fool for Christ's sake. 'Why do you not join the real Church?' he asked. Tommy was ready with his answer. The first reason was he was converted in a Methodist Chapel and there is good reason for staying with those who were converted. Secondly, Methodist religion suits Tommy. He reckoned that those who joined that Church were getting down on their knees and Tommy didn't like that. Third, the Methodist Church gives him work to do and Tommy likes preaching. The Anglican Church would not let him preach nor would the vicar let him preach at all.

Then Tommy had his last word. 'You wouldn't even let any minister preach there and he can lick all of you.'

That was the way that Samuel Chadwick was held by all the people that came to his Church. His sister, who became the wife of the Revd. W.W. Hollings, was his housekeeper, was almost driven to distraction at the way he emptied both pantry and wardrobe to assist the needy. They were fetched out at night to pray with dying folk, to settle quarrels and to stop fights. Samuel preached at every Street corner but his bitterest enemies were the publicans. He fought them at every corner and he was never afraid to remind men that the publican sent men to hell.

It was during his ministry at Wesley that Samuel Chadwick met Miss Crowther, the lady who later became his wife. She was a member of the respected family at Boston Spa and the young missioner went over on occasions to preach in the Methodist Church of that town. On the day of the wedding, crowds from Wesley went over in wagonettes to Boston Spa. When, years afterwards, from Oxford Place, Chadwick published his volume of sermons, *Humanity and God*, he included the following dedication. 'To my wife's Mother and Mine also, both of which gave me of their Best.'

Sarah Chadwick, nee Crowther

The three years at Wesley passed all too quickly, as Norman Dunning has noted.

> The Church was crowded, a revival had swept the neighbourhood, the strongholds of sin had been assailed, iniquity had been challenged in high places and the drink trade was desperately on the defensive. Gambling schools had been broken up and scores of notorious

> characteristics had been saved. Samuel Chadwick was the most loved man and the most hated man in Leeds, and his fame was in all the Churches throughout the land. As yet he was but a young man of thirty-three.[10]

After leaving Wesley in 1893, Samuel Chadwick became the minister of the Shoreditch Mission but his ministry in London only lasted for twelve months. He used to tell the story of the way he preached his first sermon with the builders' writ in his pocket. The Mission was heavily in debt but in the ministry of twelve months he inspired new hope, raised nearly seven hundred pounds and left with a balance in hand. After one year he was recalled and in 1894 returned to Leeds and was appointed Superintendent of Oxford Place. For generations it had prided itself on being the premier Methodist Chapel of the city and its pride became a problem. Its congregation of four hundred left a thousand seats unoccupied and this became a problem. The Quarterly Meeting passed a resolution that Samuel Chadwick would not be its minister but the Conference knew best. When he arrived early the following September the reception he received was anything but hearty but he was not dismayed. His success was immediate. The huge Chapel was crowded on the first Sunday morning. There was no elaborate organisation, no sensational advertisement, just prayer, and preaching and work. God did the rest. For thirteen years the crowds came and Oxford Place became the central base for the fighting forces of righteousness in Leeds.

The name of Samuel Chadwick was well known among the unchurched crowds as among the Methodists. The wolf was hunted and the city knew the hunter. The preacher captured his crowd and kept it. The existing premises were soon inadequate and in 1896 a reconstruction scheme was started and was completed in 1896 at a cost of over thirty thousand pounds. While the work was in progress, the Sunday services were held in the Coliseum. The great theatre was capable of accommodating over four thousand people but it was crowded every Sunday night and hundreds were unable to obtain

---

[10] Norman Dunning, *Samuel Chadwick*, pp.76, 77.

admission. From the stage of the Coliseum Samuel Chadwick preached steadily through Dr. Pope's *Compendium of Theology*. The congregation was drawn not only from all parts of Leeds but from neighbouring towns and villages. A train from Keighley to Leeds each Sunday evening bought so many passengers to the services that it became known as 'Chadwick's train.' When the great Anniversary meetings on Shrove Tuesday were instituted, Methodists came from all parts of Yorkshire. They would arrive at the Chapel shortly after ten o'clock in the morning. They were treated to a feast at midday. The service over, they partook of a sandwich before the meeting which commenced at three o'clock. By half-past five the Chapel was filled again for the evening meeting, and only when the mighty crowd, filling the building to the uttermost corner, stood to sing the Doxology shortly before ten o'clock, would those from far away think of their return journey. The occasion was a great spiritual festival as well as an opportunity for a financial appeal. Samuel Chadwick never begged but the people gave him all the money he needed and the proceeds of his Anniversary were seldom less than two thousand pounds.

Samuel Chadwick remembered these Leeds days with affection.

> The same converting power solved all our problems and they were neither few nor small. We had no modern accessories of missions. We just preached and prayed and worked and God did the rest. For thirteen years the crowds came and the Grace of God prevailed. We were always fighting drink, gambling and immortality. For three years there was a vigorous and fierce campaign of infidelity. One Sunday night they filled the gallery with their crowd, and that was the beginning of the end, for the ringleader was converted and every one of the leaders was captured for God..... It is difficult to stop when Leeds is my theme, but I do not write to glorify my ministry, for it was all the will of God and it is to His praise that I testify of the Grace of God.... perhaps I have said enough, though I have left so much unsaid. I love Leeds. I love its people. I love its spirit. I love everything about it.... A generation has passed since I first knew it, but my heart is still cheered by the warmth of its welcome.[11]

[11] D.W. Lambert, *The Testament of Samuel Chadwick*, pp.23-25.

For thirteen years as Pastor of Oxford Place, Samuel Chadwick's name became known all over Britain and further afield. Students from the Methodist Headingley College flocked to hear him Sunday by Sunday. His fellow-preachers used to go to his booksellers to know what books he had been reading. No Pastor was more beloved by his people. No visiting preacher held the crowd as did their own minister. One morning a postcard came from T.G. Selby. It read: 'Dear Brother Chadwick, I had a funny dreamt last night. I dream that I was conducting the Sunday Evening Service at Oxford Place and you were on the platform with me. As soon as I began to preach the people began to go out and kept on going until you came along and tapped my shoulder and said, "Stop, Selby, else in a few minutes they will be all gone." Yours affectionately, T.G. Selby. The thousands who thronged Oxford Place Sunday by Sunday were Chadwick's men and women. One Easter he was alone and invited all to come to tea with him. After the service the Secretary wanted to know how many people he should provide for and Chadwick said about half-a-dozen. Six hundred turned up! Happily the pastor had a baker among his people and the six hundred at any rate had each a little.

All through his life Chadwick was a man who was an evangelist and also a High Churchman. A poster with a big red banner advertised Passiontide Services at the Leeds Mission. Many people took offence but the Missioner knew his purpose. He was repeating the experiment made in Edinburgh. The Church was crowded night after night to hear the story of the Lord's redeeming passion. During those great days at Oxford Place, in every office and business house, on a Monday morning, Samuel Chadwick's sermon of the Sunday night was discussed. Scarcely a day passed without some miracle of conversion.

Added to the great work he was carrying in Leeds came the ever-increasing demand for Chadwick's services outside the city. His name had become a household word throughout Methodism. He was in great demand as a preacher and lecturer and he travelled Methodism from end to end, inspiring great congregation with his unique ability as a Bible expositor. Perhaps of all his great lectures was a passage in the

Book of Revelation and this was typical of Chadwick's Biblical exposition. On one occasion at Hednesford in the Cannoch Circuit, as he was delivering the lecture, he intimated, after speaking for an hour and twenty minutes, that it was time to conclude. Instantly shouts came from all parts of the Chapel, 'Go on, go on!' The Staffordshire audience felt that even an hour and twenty minutes was not long enough to listen to a lecture as that. They vigorously clamoured for more. The substance of that lecture was first published as a sermon with the title 'Sixes and Sevens.'

SIXES AND SEVENS
An Address to Working Men

'Let him that hath understanding count the number of the beast: for it is the number of a man; and his number is Six hundred threescore and six.' Rev. 13:18.

There are more bleached bones of dead theories around this verse than are about and other verse in the Bible. Hundreds of books have been written to explain the beast and its number, and to identify the man whose number is 666. There is no lack of variety; for every new interpreter suggests a different solution, and flatters himself that he has found the key to the riddle. Every possible manipulation of the figures has been tried but wise men have left it as it is. The expositors may, however, be roughly divided into two schools: (1) the historic and prophetical; (2) the mystic and symbolic.

The expositors of the former seek to locate the events, and fix their theories in history. They have suffered much at the hands of time. Nothing is so heartless as time. The unfeeling avenger has made terrible havoc among the prophets of this strange book. After endless calculation, the hero of some prophesied event is proclaimed: by some unforeseen mischance he dies without progeny.

To the mystics the Apocalypse is an allegory, a book of signs. In all symbolic teaching, it has to be remembered that the literal is not true. So is this book. Gold is not gold, crowns are not crowns, harps are not harps: these are only signs by which spiritual things are made known. Most people, however, have given up the hope of finding the wonderful beast in an individual, and a place of refuge is sought in systems. Even the French commentator Godet believes it refers to the Jewish religion, and a host of scholars find it in the Church of Rome. I have no hope of settling a question on which experts differ. We will leave the divines to settle their differences and stick to our course, trying to find out the spiritual and practical teaching of the Book.

I. The Beast whose Number is 666

The beast is not one but three. It is evident the last verse sums up the two chapters, and gives its total number like the answer in an addition sum.

1. The first beast is the 'great red dragon' of chapter 12. He has 'seven heads and ten horns, and seven crowns upon his head.' He appears in heaven in open revolt against all authority, and with special enmity against the Man-Child. War is proclaimed in heaven. The dragon had a large following, even to 'a third part of the stars of heaven.' But Michael and his angels met the rebels in pitched battle, defeated the devil, and threw him over the battlements. Heaven rejoices but earth becomes the scene of slaughter and woe. Defeated in heaven, he will triumph on earth: and proceeds to persecute the woman and her seed, by which is represented the Church of Jesus Christ. Who is this daring, determined fiend who disturbs heaven's peace, and is thirsty for the blood of saints? In verse 9 we are told he is 'that old serpent, called the devil, and Satan.' That point is clear enough at any rate; we have heard of him before.

2. The second beast rises up out of the sea, and is Daniel's four beasts rolled into one. It is part leopard, part bear, part lion, and has the ten horns 'dreadful and terrible' beast. The most remarkable feature in this monster of the sea is that one of his heads had received a fatal sword-stroke, 'and his wounds were healed.' Unto this beast the 'great red dragon,' the devil, gave his power, his throne, and great authority. He takes up the rebellion against God, heaven, and the saints, and extends his authority over all kingdoms and tongues and nations – 'The prince of this world,' a title thrice given by Jesus Christ to His adversary.

3. The third beast rises up out of the earth, and in many respects differs from its fellow-beasts. Instead of being a combination of terrors, it is meek and gentle in its appearances. It has the form of a lamb. Its mild and innocent looks are belied by its words, which carry its real character; for they are fierce, treacherous and cruel. It is the servant of the beast-

royal. It is zealous for his honour, wields his authority, works miracles for his glory, makes men worship his image, and rejoices to lose itself in the splendour and glory of its lord. This miracle-working beast works in the sphere of intellect, will, heart, and conscience, and shows 'such great signs and wonders' that they almost deceive the very elect.

Here, then, we see the great red dragon and two beasts, varying in form and sphere of operation, but one in nature and purpose. Their relationship to each other is such as to suggest at once the Evangelist's conception of a trinity of evil, in deadly conflict with the divine and holy Trinity of good. The first, a beast with seven crowned heads, claims equality with God, challenges the Most High in open rebellion, and there is war in heaven.

After the Man-Child is taken up into heaven, and the Church placed beyond the devil's reach, this fallen monarch, once almost divine, takes no direct part in the war against the saints. He relegates his authority to the beast, in whose form is represented the aggregate forces arrayed against the Kingdom of Christ. Does not this correspond to the Father's committal of all power into the hands of His only-begotten Son? Has He not placed the government upon His shoulder?

The position and sphere of the third beast corresponds in every feature to that of the Holy Ghost. What the third beast is to the second the Holy Spirit is to Jesus Christ. He toils for the spread of the Saviour's kingdom, reveals Him to the world, and by miracles and wonders moves men to worship the exalted Lord, by convincing the reason, convincing the conscience, and persuading the will. And as Father, Son, and Holy Ghost are one God, so in some way there exists in the world a trinity of evil, and the number of this trinity of beasts is 666.

II. What is the Significance of this Number 666?

The numbers are signs, and must be taken, not in their literal or numerical value, but in their symbolic sense. Here again it is important to remember three is not three, four is not four, six is not six, seven is not seven. They stand for something altogether outside arithmetic. For instance, three is a number of mysterious sanctity and refers to deities; four represents the earth in all its four corners; and six is everywhere the unlucky number. The reason given is that it is fatally below seven, the emblem of completeness, perfection, totality. Six is nearest seven, but always falls one short of completeness.

If we wrote the doctrine of the Trinity is figures, it would be 777. The Father, Son, and Holy Spirit are represented by the perfect number. The number of the beast, the trinity of evil, is 666; each beast having great authority and great power, but each falling short of completeness by one count. His number is 666. Not the number of some individual; but just as in Revelation 21:17, 'the measure of a man,' means 'human' as distinct from angelic, so I believe here the man stands as representative of his kind, and the highest point to which humanity can rise is identical with that of the beasts, and the number of man is 666.

III. That the Highest Possible Point of Attainment, apart from God, is 666.

This admits that without God 6 can be reached. We can do a great deal without God. No words are more frequently misquoted than those of our Lord, 'Without Me, ye can do nothing.' These words are absolutely true in their connection of Christian growth and fruit; but they are not true as we apply them. In Church life we can do a great deal without God. Crowded Churches and overflowing coffers are no infallible sign of the divine Presence. Filling Churches is a matter of business, not of religion; and if the Church is empty, it evidences lack of capacity rather than of piety. Given certain human conditions, any place can be filled, apart altogether from the prayer-meetings. A full Chapel does not necessarily spell success. It may be worth very little, and there may be more honour in empty pews than crowded benches. My contention is that 'sizes' can fill Chapels; that it may be due rather to religious Barnumism than the Holy Spirit. Crowds may not be Churches. Its number will only be the same as the devil's 666.

In individual reform much can be done without God. I have known men give up drink, gambling, lust, swearing, and almost every form of vice, and reform so completely that they have been held up in 'reports' as miracles of grace; and afterwards they have confessed there was no grace in it, that they had never prayed, nor sought help from God. It was only 6. The devil can go in strong for reform when it suits him; but his work lacks one thing, and that is the one thing needful. He can fetch you up to 6: it takes God to make you 7.

The most perfect systems without God leave the deepest and most vital questions of the heart unanswered. What has philosophy to answer to the first question of opening intelligence, Whence am I? What explanation can it give to my heart-hunger, my ceaseless yearning for the Infinite? What light can it throw across the chasm of death? It is mockery to talk learnedly of trifles, and be dumb to my heart's greatest need. Philosophy has no answer. It is only 6. It needs God to tell me whence I came, what I am, and whither I go. He alone can supply what lies between '6' and '7.'

This is Christ's method, and the Kingdom can be reached by no other. His is the only 7, and His 7 includes the 6, just as a shilling included the pence. His converting grace will change the hovel into a home, and sweep away the dens of pestilence and death. His Spirit will quicken the faculties and make men eager to grow in knowledge and grace. So Jesus Christ is still the only Saviour. He will reconstruct society by regenerating the individual; and the host of Christian workers, despised preachers of the Gospel, Sunday School teachers, and old-fashioned people who still go to prayer-meetings, are, after all, the best social reformers this world has. They have one complete Gospel; all others are but 666.

IV. What is your Number?

Apply this to your own life. What is your number? Is it 6 or 7? You can get a good deal out of a life of sixes. You may get a lot of real pleasure out of life without religion. I know it is the fashion to say you cannot, but unless you are a fool, you may. Given plenty of money, pleasant surroundings, brilliant companions, a man ought to be ashamed of himself if he cannot have a good time. Yet the best of the world's pleasure is only 6. The provoking thing about it is that there is always something short. It never quite satisfies. Jesus Christ said of it, 'Whosoever drinketh of this water shall thirst again;' and the more he drinks the more he thirsts. But He gives the water of life that leaves no thirst; and, after all, you never know what happiness is till you drink of that stream.

In character too you may be good without Christ. I admit it; but your goodness is only 6. A fine specimen of the '6' order came to Jesus one day. He had kept the Commandments; he was greatly respected; so excellent was he, that when Jesus saw him 'He loved him.' But He said unto him, 'One thing thou lackest.' Only one, but it was the one thing needful.

When I preached this sermon in my Church in Leeds, a young fellow was present who had not been attending a place of worship. During the appeal I remember looking at him and wondering how much of my sermon he had got. It was sacrament night, and, as he was not a member, I had no further opportunity of urging decision. On the Thursday he fell ill. On Friday he was worse, on Saturday the doctor came and on Sunday morning he pronounced him dying. At noon I was sent for. Immediately my feet touched the stairs he called on me to pray. 'Pray right hard,' he said, 'remember I am dying.' I prayed. 'Pray again,' he cried; 'pray right hard.' I prayed again. When I got up from my knees he said, 'Sing! Sing, Jesus Lover of my soul.' We tried to sing, and broke down choked with tears. 'Don't cry,' he said; 'Sing! Sing!' After we had sung, he asked for prayer again. Then, taking my hand in his, and looking at me for the first time, he said: 'I shall never hear you preach any more – never, never any more. I didn't think last Sunday it would be the last time, but it was. I shall never hear you again.' He lay silent for a few minutes, for he was fast failing. Then looking up with a smile, he said, 'But it's 777.' 'Not 6,' sobbed his broken-hearted mother. 'No,' he replied; 'I am going where there no sixes; it's 777.' Again he said, 'Sing! Sing the Doxology.' He gave out the words, and joined himself in the hymn of praise. Then his strength failed. Drawing my face to his, he kissed my cheek, and whispered, 'It's 777.' In twenty minutes he was dead. His soul had passed beyond all that is animal and sensuous, beyond all that is of the earth, earthy. He had passed within the gate into the city, and his last word was, 'It's 777.'

During his sixteen years in Leeds, the profile of Samuel Chadwick grew and grew and he was known all over England as one of Methodism's greatest preachers. He was invited to attend Methodist worship and preaching classes and his style was known everywhere. At the first Sunday in the year 1903, a few friends were sitting near the fire in his home and the conversation turned on why he didn't publish his sermons. Chadwick replied that it would be an open call from God and he didn't have that call. Then Chadwick brings the story up to date.

> Then I was asked what I would regard as a call of God. I answered at once and without much thought. 'An unsolicited request from Hodder and Stoughton.' The subject dropped, as the condition was thought unreasonable. Within twenty-four hours the request came. No one had communicated with the publishers and there was only one possible answer. The sermons selected were preached from notes as a series in the regular course of my ministry. An underlying unity runs through the series, yet each sermon had to be practically complete in itself. Through an exceptionally busy life I have striven to give attention to reading, and what I've read has passed into the fibre and substance of my work.... My only prayer concerning them is, that they may be blessed in print as they were blessed in speech, and that Christ's Name may be glorified.[12]

Humanity and God has seventeen sermons and covers the area that grace makes known to man. The second sermon, *Sin and Grace*, is based on the text, 'Where sin abounded, grace did abound more exceedingly,' (Rom. 5:20). Sin and grace are the two great words of the Christian religion and lie at the very heart of the Gospel of Christ. The Epistle to the Romans has come to be regarded as the very core of the Gospel, because it deals so completely with those fundamental words. The sin of Adam involved the whole race in ruin; the righteousness of Christ restored men and women to the justification of life. The act of the one is the act of all, and the results of the act are shared by all. The contrast is set forth in the five times 'much more' of the chapter. The disobedience of Adam spread over the whole race; the obedience of Christ gathered the sins of all unto Himself. From Paradise there went forth the stream of death; from Calvary there flows the river of life. The grace of God in Christ has cancelled sin and destroyed the works of the devil. Grace has abounded over sin.

The Bible always deals with man as a sinful being. The fact of sin explains the process of Divine Revelation and the whole economy of Redemption. The Law came to make sin manifest and to correct man's transgressions. Every part of the sacred ordinances proceeded on the assumption of man's guilt and his need of cleansing. If man be not

---

12 Samuel Chadwick, *Humanity and God*, 'A Personal Word', pp.vii -ix.

sinful, the whole Scripture is without meaning and the Gospel a delusion.

> The Book that gives unique distinction to man in his creation, tells of his transgression and humiliation. According to its account man failed to attain his destiny. He grasped at divinity by forbidden means and fell from his high estate. The bond of fellowship with the Divine was broken, and from kinship with God he fell to kinship with Satan. His understanding was darkened and his heart hardened. From the realm of the spirit he descended to that of the flesh. The symmetry of his nature was broken and its order reversed. Instead of unity there was conflict within him. That which should have governed became captive, and that which was meant for service assumed control. Confusion took the place of harmony, and chaos succeeded a well-ordered cosmos.[13]

The Bible does not concern itself with the fall but with the fallen. It comes not to explain but to emancipate, not to philosophise but to save. It explains only where the explanation is deemed necessary to salvation. Stripped of all accessories of allegorical speech, the simple account is that sin entered through the acceptance of evil by the free will of man. Whatever the circumstances, this is the inner reality – man chose evil. There can be no other explanation of the ultimate fact. Without the free choice there could have been no sin. After all the searching criticism of the Genesis story, in all its essentials, it stands as the only rational and adequate explanation of evil that is in man, and his consequent need of redemption.

We are on sure ground when we come to the scriptures for the answer as to its nature and consequences. John defines human conflict; 'sin is the transgression of the law' (1 John 3:4). That is the final definition. It tracts sin to its innermost secret, and comprehends all the facts of its manifold operations. Sin is not an act but an attitude. The offence is not only in the transgression but in the intention; not merely in the violation of law but in the disposition of the heart. Christ emphasised this in the Sermon on the Mount. Anger is murder in malice and motive. Lust is adultery though it never pass beyond the look of desire. The seat of sin is in the will. Man is not a sinner because he is a

---

13 Samuel Chadwick, *Sin and Grace*, 1903, pp.23, 24.

transgressor; he is a transgressor because he is a sinner. The sin of lawlessness precedes the act of transgression. Disobedience in act is the effect of which lawlessness is the cause.

As sin is the cause of all sins, so death is the sum of all its consequences. 'The wages of sin is death' (Rom. 6:23). That something more than physical death is meant, is evidence both from the narrative in Genesis, and in the Scriptural use of the word. When man sinned he died. Men are said to be dead while they live. Sin slays the man made in the Divine image. Guilt, disorder and desolation are the marks of the soul's death. God holds the sinner responsible for his sin. Wickedness lays waste all things beautiful and good. It turns Paradise into a wilderness and Heaven into Hell. It is in the heart and in the world as a loathsome pestilence. Sin is the most terrible thing in God's universe. We have all sinned and there is not one sinless among us. The only prayer that becomes our lips is: 'God be merciful to me a sinner' (Luke 18:13).

> Over against this terrible word sin, stands the greater word Grace. This conjunction of the two defines the limits of our consideration of the word which comprehends the Evangelical faith. Grace goes over the trail of sin, tracks it to its innermost recesses, destroys its power, undoes its mischief, and turns its very weapons to its own destruction. Grace not only conquers, it more than conquers; it not only abounds, it abounds more exceedingly. We are saved by grace. What is grace? There is no definition of grace as there is of sin. It defies definition. It is illimitable, infinite, eternal. It is illustrated but never defined. In this connexion it is the overflowing mercy of God, without regard to merit on the one hand or obligation on the other. We had no claim. Our sin had forfeited every right we ever possessed. God was under no obligation. We had defined His authority, rejected His word, and voluntarily forsaken Him for His sworn foe. But of His mercy He saved us. 'God commendeth His own love toward us, in that, while we were yet sinners, Christ died for us' (Rom. 5:8). Grace redeemed, delivered, and restored man from the curse and dominion of sin. The overtures did not come from man but from God. From first to last, salvation is of the grace of God.[14]

[14] Samuel Chadwick, *Sin and Grace*, pp.30, 31.

Grace is peculiarly associated with the mediatorial work of our Lord Jesus Christ. It is in the sacrifice of the Cross it finds its highest expression. Grace comes to us through Him. Sin finds its destruction in His death. The Cross is meaningless apart from sin. The Scriptures leave us in no doubt that to save men from sin, it was necessary that Christ should die. His death was vicarious and sacrificial. He was 'The Lamb of God which takes away the sin of the world' (John 1:29). Sin laid the sinner under the wrath and condemnation of God. It separated from God and destroyed the basis of fellowship, which was identity of life. Before man could be restored, sin's penalty must be paid. A way must be found by which God could be just, and the justifier of the ungodly; a way by which man could be restored not only to the possibility of fellowship, but to the moral and spiritual fitness for it. That problem was solved in Jesus Christ the Eternal Son of the Father. It is the burden of the Gospel that He died for our sins. He gathered unto Himself and bore in His own Person the sin of the whole world. Every sinner may look to the Cross and say, 'He loved me and He gave Himself up for me' (Gal. 2:20).

Bearing shame and scoffing rude
In my place condemned He stood
Sealed my pardon with His blood
Alleluia! What a Saviour!

Philip Bliss[15]

The ambassadors of the Gospel are sent to proclaim the forgiveness of sin. Without exception and without condition we are sent to tell every sinner that Jesus Christ has made Atonement for the world's sin, and through Him is preached the forgiveness for sinners. How difficult it is to persuade men and women that the Good News is not reserved for worthy and respectable people! It is for prodigals, outcasts, wanderers; for every one that answers the description and title of sinners. The Lord came, not to call the righteous but sinners to repentance. Every barrier is removed, every obligation met, every sin cancelled, every sinner forgiven; the Gospel is a message of a full, free, and universal pardon,

[15] Philip Bliss, *The Methodist Hymn-Book*, 1904.

on no other conditions than such as are involved in its acceptance through Christ.

Samuel Chadwick saves his last exhortation to the end.

> The restored order in the man secures the restoration of the true order in the world. The new man necessitated a New Heaven and a New Earth. Personal regeneration is followed by social reconstruction. Sin brought guilt, grace brings justification; sin separated man from God, grace brings him nigh by the blood of Christ; sin darkened the understanding and defiled the heart, grace brings light and knowledge and purifies the heart; sin disturbed the true order of man's nature and defaced the Divine image within him, grace creates him anew after the image of God in righteousness and true holiness; sin cursed the world, grace restores its peace and blessing; sin brought death, grace brings the gift of life. Wherever sin abounded, grace has abounded more exceedingly. There are still the two Adams, and the responsibility of choice still lies with man. We can reject grace and continue in sin, or we may renounce sin and live in grace. Every man and woman elects to be identified with Adam or Christ, to choose sin or grace. No man need continue in sin, for grace has abounded unto complete salvation.

The second sermon chosen from, *Humanity And God,* is, 'The Way Of The Cross,' based on Matt. 16:24; 'Then Jesus said to His disciples, "If any man would come after Me, let him deny himself, and take up his cross, and follow Me." Whatever Christ's previous consciousness may have been, there can be no doubt as to the significance of this crisis. It marks a new departure. There is another tone in His speech, a marked straitening of soul, and a distinct focussing of interest and activity. The Cross was His one theme, and the accomplishment of its Sacrifice His supreme passion. The chapters from 4:17 to 16:20 contain the record of Christ's preaching of the Kingdom. Its principles are stated, expounded, and applied, and its promises set forth, in parable, miracle, argument and instruction.

Just as the Cross was the Christ's only way to the Eternal priesthood, so it is the disciples' only way to realised salvation. He saw the essence of worldliness and a temptation of the devil. The wisdom of the world is self-sparing, self-shielding, self-seeking. Spare yourself is the sum of its philosophy and its invariable policy. The doctrine of the Kingdom is not spare but sacrifice. To shirk the Cross is to miss the Kingdom. The peculiarity of the Christian life is symbolised in the Cross.

> It was an alien judgement pursuing him even unto death. He stands condemned by the power of an alien. The world hated Christ and killed Him. They are still in antagonism. He who would be with Christ must come out from the world and share His reproach and condemnation. If the world crucified Christ, it will not be more tolerant of His followers. He warned us to expect for ourselves the treatment it gave to Him..... It was here the rich young Ruler found his Cross. The Lord laid upon him the stern and apparently prohibitive condition, 'If you would be perfect, go, sell that thou hast, and give to the poor, and thou shalt have treasure in Heaven; and come, follow Me. But when the young man heard the saying, he went away sorrowful for he was one that had great possessions' (Matt. 19:22). This was his Cross, and he, shrinking, spared himself, and was lost to the Kingdom. The Cross is inevitable. No man can love the world and follow Christ.[16]

If we are called to the fellowship of His sufferings, as well as to partnership in His service, the essential features of motive and work must be the same in us as in Him. What does that mean in practical life? It means that the man who takes up the Cross and follows Christ lives in the will of God for the service of man. He is God's steward, and the sphere of his stewardship is in the sin and sorrow of the world. This is bearing the Cross; sorrowing over the world's sin, bearing the world's burden, carrying the world's shame, ministering to the world's need, laying down our life for the world's salvation. This is the badge and test of discipleship. Have we taken up the Cross? Have we dared to come out of the world, antagonised ourselves to it, and borne its reproach? Are we surrendered in all things to the will of God? Do we weep over it, pray for it, live for it, die for it? It is for these the Cross stands, and without the Cross we cannot be Christ's disciples.

The Cross supplies both the weapon and the method for the conversion of the world to Christ. Because Christianity is life it cannot be

---

16 Samuel Chadwick, *The Way of the Cross*, pp.121, 122.

imposed; it can only be imparted. Life can only extend by propagation. Every soul has to be begotten. Souls born of God are begotten of the Spirit and of the Word, and the vehicle of quickening truth is found in living souls. Living saints bring dead sinners to life. The conquest of revival waits on a quickened Church. When the Church is passionless the world is indifferent. So once again, it is the Gospel of the Cross. There is no salvation but by blood. We too must die if we would not abide alone. Every true revival begins with a revived realisation of the Cross. The Missionary spirit is born at Calvary. It is at the Cross the Evangel is born and by the Cross it prevails.

Samuel Chadwick was at his best when it comes to finishing a living word from God.

> There is only one Gospel for all peoples. The one Cross draws all men. The Cross draws the cultured Greek, conquers the Roman warrior, and allures the Hebrew. The Cross is the way to Pentecost. The Spirit was not given till the Cross was accomplished and the Son of Man was glorified. The disciple must die with Christ to be baptised with the Holy Ghost and with fire. The Cross! The Cross! Always the Cross! It is the way to God. In it, through it, by it, is everything that saves, sanctifies, and glorifies the soul of man. It is the way to purity, it is the way to power, it is the way to Pentecost, it is the way to service, it is the way to glory.[17]

Chadwick's third sermon is *Christian Perfection*, and the passage is, 'This we also pray for you, your perfection' (2 Cor. 13:9). There is probably no subject Christian teachers touch so reluctantly as that of Christian Perfection. This is due partly to the difficulties, and partly to the fact that it lays open to misunderstanding. A still deeper reason for reluctance is the conscious gulf that lies between the doctrine and experience. It is not easy to urge others to perfection while our lives fall short; and it is easy to take refuge in the differences and inconsistencies of those who profess it, and hold our peace. Such silence is neither courageous nor guiltless; for while there may be but little hope of agreement in definition, there can be no doubt the

---

[17] Samuel Chadwick, *The Way of the Cross,* p.133.

Scriptures speak of a perfection that is both attainable and imperative. The Scriptures command perfection, promise perfection, and give examples of perfection. God does not mock us with impossible commands. Noah, Abraham, and Job are all spoken of as perfect before God, and Paul exhorts the perfect in his Philippians letter.

All the elements of Christian character are set forth in the scriptures as capable of perfection. The elements that make up Christian character are faith, hope and love.

1. Faith. Paul writes to the Thessalonians and says: 'Night and day praying exceedingly that we may see your face, and may perfect that which is lacking in your faith' (1 Thess. 3:10). Their faith was deficient. It lacked something, but whatever it was in which they fell short, it was capable of being supplied. Whatever the process of perfection, the perfect is possible. Life may be lived without doubt, without wavering, and without unbelief. At all times and in all things, the heart may be fully assured in the truth and will of God.

2. Hope. Faith plants its feet securely upon the certainties of the word. It examines, proves, and stakes everything upon assured truth. It builds on the rock. It dwells in the future. Its home is within the veil. Though billows and darkness be on every side, hope soars above them all, and out-flying the storm, dwells in the calm of eternal day. This living hope may be set perfectly on the grace that is to be revealed at the revelation of Jesus Christ.

3. Love. 'Herein is love made perfect, that we may have boldness in the day of judgement, because as He is, even so are we in this world' (I John 4, 17, 18).

> Love made perfect! Heart, soul, and mind cleansed from every defilement, united and harmonised, every part enthused with holy fervour and reverent devotion. When love is perfect there is no fear because there is no sense of guilt, no unrest because no strife, no coldness because no sin. The soul made perfect in love is delivered from all that separated it from God and divided man's nature against itself. It is restored and sanctified, renewed and adjusted, cleansed and filled with

> the presence of God. Love reigns, love radiates, love inspires, love transforms. Love is the sum of duty and the inspiration of life. Perfect faith; perfect hope; perfect love; these make the perfect man in the stature of the fullness of Christ.[18]

The perfection of faith, hope and love bears fruit unto perfection in the graces of the Christian life. Does the perfection of grace in the soul result in perfection in the practical out-working of the daily life? Christian perfection does not mean faultlessness but blamelessness. It does not mean that a thing has reached the excellence beyond which there is no possibility of improvement, but that the work is perfect in motive, and perfect according to the capacity of the worker. That an act is perfect in this sense implies that it is simple in aim and faithful in execution. So with the Christian graces in the man or woman made perfect. They lack no essential quality, and are adequate to the strain that is put upon them.

'Let patience have its perfect work, that you may be perfect and entire, lacking in nothing' (James 1:4). Patience is the child of the three graces. The secret of patience is love, hopefulness, and confidence. Where any one of these elements is lacking patience will be wanting, but where these are, patience will have its perfect work. The Christian made perfect in faith, hope and love will be perfect in his patience with God. Though the Kingdom of God come slowly and all things seem to continue as they were, we know that He who cannot lie has sworn to His Son that He shall have the nations for His inheritance, and the uttermost parts of the earth for His possession; and though we see not yet all things subjected to Him, we see Jesus crowned with glory and honour. In this vision faith rests, hope sings, and love waits.

Holiness is the objective of grace. Adjustment and cleansing, Divine indwelling and inworking are all for the purpose of holiness of heart and righteousness of life. Goodness is the goal of all God's working. Faith is made perfect by its works; hope purifies by its vision; and love not only keeps the commandments but sets them to music. Perfect and

---

[18] Samuel Chadwick, *Christian Perfection*, pp.255, 256.

fully assured in all the will of God; perfect, furnished completely unto every good work; perfect, in every good thing to do His will. Christian perfection means that a man lives in the assurance of God's approval; that he is equipped and abounds in good works, and that his outward life is inspired and energised by an indwelling and inworking God. The soul made perfect in grace dwells in God and obeys His will. Business, friendship, home, pleasure, and all else are adjusted to His mind and maintained according to His pleasure. Such perfect obedience is only possible to perfect faith, perfect hope, and perfect love; but to faith, hope, and love all things are possible.

> To-day the Saviour looks and challenges us to perfection. 'If you would be perfect' (Matt. 19:21). The very 'if' assumes the possibility. Perfection is neither by the law of Moses, nor by the law of the Sanctuary. It is the work and gift of God, and can only become ours by consecration, cleansing and indwelling. 'If you would be perfect, go, sell what you have, and give to the poor.' That is the first great commandment of the perfect life: absolute and unconditional surrender of the whole life to God.... The life is not the life of the perfect man, but of the perfect Christ who dwells and works in the soul by His Spirit. It is God's work. It is the work of the perfect Worker, and everyone whom He perfects shall be as his Master. 'Faithful is He that calls you, who will also do it' (I Thess. 5:24). When He has done it, we need not proclaim it, for perfection, above all things, cannot be hid. 'Now the God of peace, who brought again from the dead the great Shepherd of the sheep, with the blood of the eternal covenant, even our Lord Jesus, make you perfect in every good thing to do His will, working in you that which is well-pleasing in His sight, through Jesus Christ, to whom be glory for ever and ever' (Heb. 13:20, 21), Amen.[19]

The fourth sermon under consideration is entitled, *The Christian Benediction,* and comes from 2 Cor. 13:14; 'The grace of the Lord Jesus Christ, and the love of God, and the communion of the Holy Ghost, be with you all.' Christ's reception of the Spirit was the call and equipment of God for His Messianic ministry. Baptism into the Name means baptism unto God, and the Name of God in the new covenant is Father, Son, and Holy Spirit. He ordained it for all time to be the

---

[19] Samuel Chadwick, *Christian Perfection*, p.267.

initiating confession of faith for all who would enter His kingdom. It is the formula with which all believers are to be received into the fellowship of Christ, and like all such formulae it sets forth the fundamental doctrine of the Christian ecclesia. It is the basis of all Christian doctrine and the universal confession of the Christian faith. 'I believe in God the Father.... and in Jesus Christ His only Son our Lord .... I believe in the Holy Ghost.' Three Persons, One God. This grace sums up the blessings of Christian privilege in the three great words of the Gospel; Grace, Love, and Communion. In the economy of Redemption, Grace comes to us through Jesus, Love is of the Father, and Communion by the Holy Ghost.

> 'The grace of our Lord Jesus Christ.' The word grace is Paul's token in every Epistle. It is more than mercy and greater than love. Grace seeks the unfit and the unworthy. It is love, mercy, and compassion stretching out towards the guilty, ungracious and rebellious. It is the only hope for sinful men. If salvation come not by grace, it can never be ours. Without grace there can be no reconciliation, no pardon, no peace. We are saved by grace. It was by the grace of God Jesus Christ tasted death for every man and woman and to whom they owe their salvation. It began in grace, is continued in grace, and is perfected in grace. At no stage is it of works; it is a gift of God, the outflowing of His grace. We are commanded to 'grow in the grace and knowledge of our Lord and Saviour Jesus Christ' (2 Pet. 3:18). This passage speaks of the Divine influence in the soul as the operation of grace, and regard that which has its source in the grace of God as the working power of salvation. Grace pardons the guilty, restores the fallen, delivers the captive, sanctifies the sinner, sustains and perfects the believer.[20]

This grace is always connected with our Lord Jesus Christ. He is the manifestation of God, full of grace and truth. The love of God is revealed to men in the grace of Christ, and the grace of God will be for ever the grace of Christ. That is why His Name takes precedence in the form of blessing. The manifestation of grace is through the Man Christ Jesus. It is made known to us in His life of sinless obedience, His ministry of compassion, His suffering and death. It is through the grace

---

20 Samuel Chadwick, *The Christian Benediction*, p.347.

of God embodied and revealed in Christ that we come to the knowledge of the Father.

'And the love of God.' The Christian revelation concerning Him is that He is Love. From everlasting to everlasting God is Love. It was Eternal Love that gave the gift of the Eternal Son. Christ brings us to the Father, and makes known to us the love of God. Realisation of the love of God in the redeeming work of grace brings the conscious experience of the love of God to the soul. The love of God is shed abroad in the heart through the Holy Ghost. It is useless to attempt to define or describe the consciousness of love, for it passes knowledge. It cannot be known except through personal knowledge. The secret of love is revealed only to love. 'God is love, and he that abides in love abides in God, and God abides in him' (1 John 4:16). Love is peculiarly attributed to God, as grace is associated with Jesus Christ, though it is of the love of Christ it is said that 'it passeth knowledge,' and God is called the God of grace.

'And the communion of the Holy Ghost.' The Spirit is always revealed as the immediate Agent in the communication of God to the soul. It is He who convicts and converts, assures and inspires, equips and strengthens. In the Christian kingdom He is the Paraclete, who abides with us for ever. The communion of the Holy Ghost means partnership with Him. We share with Him the things of God. Salvation is the work of both man and God. Man works out his own salvation, but the Spirit works in him both the willing and the doing of the Divine good pleasure. The work of the kingdom is the united work of redeemed men and the Spirit of God. We are workers together with Him. He clothes Himself with men, takes possession of their powers, and through them works mightily in the world for the destruction of sin and the glory of Christ. This is the Benediction of God to man: grace, love and communion. Grace through Jesus Christ, love from God, and communion with the Holy Ghost.

In the last of his seventeen sermons, Samuel Chadwick makes much of the blessing of three-in-one. 'The grace of the Lord Jesus Christ, and the love of God, and the communion of the Holy Ghost, be with you all' (2 Cor. 12:14). This benediction sums up the blessing of Christian privilege in the three great words of the Gospel – Grace, Love, Communion. These three gifts of God are attributed to different Persons in the Trinity. Grace is attributed to our Lord Jesus Christ, Love to God, and Communion to the Holy Ghost. These distinctions interpret Christian experience, and are necessary to its existence.

'The grace of our Lord Jesus Christ.' The word grace is Paul's token in every Epistle. It leads to the consciousness of love and the life of communion; it is the great word of the Gospel of Christ. It is love, mercy, and compassion stretching out towards the guilty, ungracious and rebellious. It is the only hope for sinful men and women. If salvation come not by grace, it can never be ours. Without grace, there can be no reconciliation, no pardon, no peace. We are saved by grace. It was by the grace of God Jesus Christ tasted death for every man, and it is to the same grace every man owes his salvation. It begins in grace, is continued in grace, and is perfected in grace. At no stage is it of works; it is a gift of God, the out-flowing of His grace.

In the New Testament use of the word it passes from an attribute of the Divine character to an active energy in the soul. At the Throne of Grace we 'find grace to help us in time of need' (Heb. 4:6). The heart is 'established by grace' (Heb. 13:9), and by grace 'we may offer service well-pleasing to God' (Heb. 12:28). It is in 'the grace that is in Christ Jesus' (2 Tim. 2:1), that we find our strength, and we are assured of its sufficiency for endurance as well as for service. 'My grace is sufficient for thee' (2 Cor. 12:9). We are commanded to 'grow in the grace and knowledge of our Lord and Saviour Jesus Christ' (2 Pet. 3:18). These passages all speak of the Divine influence in the soul as the operation of grace, and regard that which has its power in the grace of God as the working power of salvation. Grace pardons the guilty, restores the fallen, delivers the captive, sanctifies the sinner, sustains and perfects the believer. The manifestation of grace is through the Man Christ Jesus. It is made known to us in His life of sinless obedience, His ministry of compassion, His sufferings and death. It is through the grace of God embodied and revealed in Christ that we come to the knowledge of the Father.

'*And the love of God.*' He is contemplated in the completeness of His Being, and the Name is used which includes all relationships. The Christian revelation concerning Him is that He is Love. From everlasting to everlasting God is Love. It was Eternal Love that gave the gift of the Eternal Son. The love of God is shed abroad in the heart through the Holy Ghost. It cannot be known except through personal experience. The secret of love is revealed only to love. Every one that receives the grace knows the love. 'And we know and have believed the love which God hath in us. God is love; and he that abideth in love abideth in God, and God abideth in him' (1 John 4:16).

'*And the communion of the Holy Ghost.*' Grace leads to love, and love opens the way to communion. The Spirit is always revealed as the immediate Agent in the communication of God to the soul. It is He who convicts and converts, assures and inspires, equips and strengthens. In the Christian kingdom He is the Paraclete, who abides with us for ever. His abiding presence in the soul is the result of accepted grace and realised love. This is the Benediction of God to man: Grace, Love and Communion. Grace through Jesus Christ, love from God, and communion with the Holy Spirit. This is the order of the Divine process. Through Christ to God and through both to the abiding presence of the Spirit; through grace to love, and through love to the life of Divine communion.

The grace by which Jesus Christ tasted death for every man is intended to produce a like spirit of sacrifice in us. 'Because He laid down His life for us, we ought to lay down our lives for the brethren' (1 John 3:16). If the grace of the Lord Jesus Christ be with us, it will work in us as it worked in Him. The God of love dwells in us so that we may live the life of Godlike love. The companionship, partnership, and co-operation into which He brings us is intended to send us forth with like privileges to others. The threefold Benediction is to abide with us that its threefold grace may be manifested in us, and the presence of its

Three-One God demonstrated through us. All are included in the blessing, and none are omitted from the purpose.

Samuel Chadwick closes the book with a blessing on all who read it.

> The Benediction defines the mission of the Church of God. It is a family gathering of the Brotherhood of Christ where all other considerations disappear. They dwell in the love of God, and from the beginning the reality of both the grace and love has been demonstrated in the spirit of loving and practical fellowship. Grace, love and communion are the signs of the Divine Presence in the Christian Church. The message of the Church to the world is the message of the Benediction. Its gospel is a gospel of grace to the lost; the burden of its message is the love of God; and it calls all men and women to the communion of the Spirit and the fellowship of them that believe. The grace of the Lord Jesus Christ, and the love of God, and the communion of the Holy Ghost; that is the Gospel and the power by which the world is to be restored and saved. Man finds his destiny in an Indwelling Divinity and in the practice of the Divine qualities of Grace, Love, and Communion. This is man's way to his destined divinity: The grace of the Lord Jesus Christ, and the love of God, and the communion of the Holy Ghost, be with you all. Amen.[21]

The sale of the sermons astounded the public and Hodder and Stoughton wrote upon the fly-leaf: 'These sermons are soul-stirring and work-inspiring. Hundreds have received new courage and inspiration through the reading of these great sermons.' Chadwick had put into his message the power that helped people and even the written word called forth his praise. Wherever he went he held people by his word and during the great years of his ministry.

Sixteen years were spent in Leeds and every year saw many more converted to God and joining his church. From the beginning Samuel had a fondness for Cliff College in Derbyshire. Thomas Champness was the first to recognise Chadwick's ministry and in the third issue of *Joyful News* there appeared Chadwick's first article. When Champness was no longer able to contribute, Chadwick succeeded him as Editor. On March 23, Chadwick preached at the opening of Cliff College, and

[21] Samuel Chadwick, *The Christian Benediction*, pp.355, 356.

he went there every Monday morning to give lectures to the students. It soon became evident that the work at Cliff would be the next sphere of service for the great Missionary from Leeds. The Church at Oxford Place was deeply troubled and the city was dismayed by the loss of its famous preacher. However, little by little, the will of God became clear. So Chadwick declared that the Sunday he would resign and that came on August 18, 1907. Morning and evening Oxford Place was crowded and the congregation took matters into their own hands.

> A man jumped to his feet to tell two thousand people how he was brought into the light as, burdened with sin, he listened to Mr. Chadwick's preaching. Testimony followed testimony, song succeeded song, until the time of the regular service. Meanwhile scores of people were striving in vain for admission to the Chapel, literally packed from floor to ceiling, overflowing into the aisles, within the communion rail, and on the pulpit steps. Through the open door, faces new and old could be seen – men and women anxious to pay their respects, and to hear again the voice of the man from whom, for sixteen years, had 'sounded out the word of the Lord' in Leeds. Farther back on the Chapel steps and away into the Town Hall Square, there stood many who had no prospect of hearing a word of the service.[22]

At half-past six Samuel Chadwick entered the pulpit. With one voice the vast throng of two thousand five hundred people proclaimed their faith.

> Jesus shall reign, where'er the sun
> Doth his successive journeys run.
>
> Issac Watts

As Chadwick leads his congregation to the throne of grace, to the ends of the church, one feels the presence of God and experiences that strange, indefinable thrill which is a sure sign of evidence of the Spirit of God. As the Pastor prays his voice rings clear in the massive audience: 'Lord, pour out Thy blessing upon this city – its Mayor, its magistrates, its scavengers, its postmen, its policemen.' The valedictory sermon is based upon the words, 'The Gospel which I

---

[22] Norman Dunning, *Samuel Chadwick*, pp.107, 108.

preached unto you' (1 Cor. 15:1). The deep, abiding notes will last a long time in the eager listening crowd, and he tells his people of the kind of Gospel he had preached during his time there. 'If this be my last word in the name of my Master,' he said, 'I could say with all due solemnity and earnestness, there is no other Gospel, there is no other Saviour. But if you reject this Gospel of Jesus Christ you will be lost, you will be damned, and that for ever.' More than a thousand stay behind, and sinners openly testify their anxiety to be saved. From all parts of the Chapel they hurry to the enquiry rooms. What was a wonderful and glorious night is the announcement that twenty-five persons have received Christ.

Samuel Chadwick knew in his own heart that he was called to Cliff College. His own career was his great qualification for the task to which Conference had called him. His own educational advantages had been slender and from the age of fifteen he studied until midnight and was up at six to go to the mill. Through these years he had studied and vowed that if he ever found a youth who had no education, he was bound to help him. Cliff College brought him into touch with these students who had little advantage and he set himself to aid these people into ministry. The students were all local preachers and they were seeking better equipment for their Christian work. Many of them had saved for years and placed their hard-earned money at the hands of the Principal that they might have instruction and inspiration. Samuel felt as he entered Cliff College that here was a ministry that he could help and with the might of the ministry he had exercised for sixteen years at Leeds.

He was placed in charge of Homiletics and the students felt here was a man who knew his Bible and was versed in its interpretation. The clinic showed here was a man one could follow and the Canon of Homiletics went on after Chadwick's death.

Canons Of Homiletics

1. Fidelity:
   Grammar
   History
   Exegesis
2. Unity:
   The unique truth
   The theme
   The unique truth to govern and unify the whole
   The unique truth should be the title of the sermon

3. Order:
   Division should be:
   Short
   Simple
   Progressive
   Comprehensive

4. Rules:
   Relevant
   Credible
   Obvious
   Proportionate

5. Aim:
   Definitely
   Instruction
   Persuasion

6. Delivery:
   Natural
   Reverent
   Earnest

There are two sermons that have appeared again and again and it is helpful to look at them.

Buried Alive

'And when He was come forth upon the land, there met Him a certain man out of the city, who had devils; and for a long time he had worn no clothes, and abode not in any house, but in the tombs' (Luke 8:27).

Introduction: This man is a fair representation of sepulchred humanity. The problem of devil-possession humanity meets us at every turn.

1. What the Devil did for him – they stripped him:

   Of his clothes:
   Of his home:
   Of his manhood – this the master-stroke of the devil

2. What Society did for him – it cast him out:
   Caught and bound him
   Drove him into the wilderness

3. What Jesus did for him – He lifted him up:
   He showed him sympathy
   He struck at the root – turned the devils out-flying
   He clothed him
   He sent him home

Application – The story of this man is the story of to-day. The devil still strips, Christ still saves, the devil still ruins, Christ still restores.

Christian Fellowship

'That which we have seen and heard declare we unto you, that ye also may have fellowship with us: yea, and our fellowship is with the Father, and with His Son Jesus Christ' (1 John 1:3).

Introduction: Fellowship, peculiar note of the epistle

1. The Meaning of Fellowship:
   Mutual interest
   Mutual devotion
   Mutual activity

2. The Basis of Fellowship:
   Historical testimony

Experimental testimony
Real necessity

3. The Nature of Fellowship:
   With the Father
   With the Son
   With the Saints

Application – The Implication of Fellowship
1. As to inheritance – 'All things are yours'
2. As to obligations – 'If we saw .... we ought also.'

The five years passed so quickly at Cliff College and Samuel Chadwick prepared himself for something new. A new coalfield had been opened in South Yorkshire but the organisation inside Methodism was unable to cope with the new inflow. The Conference decided to free Chadwick from all other word and he was the first Superintendent of the South Yorkshire Coalfields Mission. He left Cliff in September 1912 and made his home in Sheffield, but within three weeks Thomas Cook had died and Chadwick was recalled to become Principal of Cliff College. He stayed on in Sheffield and directed the work of the College. At Conference, in the following July, his old friend, Josiah Mee, succeeded him at Sheffield and Samuel Chadwick went into residence as Principal of Cliff. It was foreseen that Chadwick would follow Thomas Cook and there was a great delight that he was the man. He had known it in all its stages and he was the ideal Principal. He was ready and possessed all the gifts and graces that made him the very man to preside over Cliff College. His personality ensured discipline and behaviour and no man dared to take liberties with Samuel Chadwick.

When he was settled in Cliff College, a student much older than an average Cliff man knocked at the door of the Principal's study. He was told that the students had to give up tobacco but he wondered if Mr. Chadwick would give him leave. He was dying for a smoke but the Principal cut him short. 'Sit down in that chair and die.' He went on to explain that the man who used tobacco was dead if he couldn't get it. The student glanced at the floor and then at the ceiling. The Principal said to him, 'Let us talk to God about this,' and he knelt on the floor beside the student. Then Mr. Chadwick prayed that God would glorify Himself in this man's life. The student rose from his knees and from that hour the craving was gone. When word about this got round the College, no man ever again dared to go to the Principal's office.

Eleven months after Chadwick had settled in Cliff College war broke out. The College was closed and three times it was commandeered by the Government but never occupied. On November 10, 1882, Thomas Champness, who was then doing the work of a District Evangelist, received a letter from Revd. Charles Garrett, who was President of the Conference, outlining a plan for a new weekly paper. On Thursday, February 22, 1883, the first *Joyful News* was published. Champness encouraged Chadwick to write and so from the first Chadwick was acquainted with *Joyful News.* Following 1903, Champness became a Supernumerary, *Joyful News* was taken over by the Wesleyan Home Mission Committee and two years later it was transferred to the Revs. H.T. Smart, Thomas Cook and Samuel Chadwick. Chadwick contributed two articles every week; the *Leader*, which appeared on the front page, which was full of sound doctrine, and the *Letter*, which was full of wisdom and thousands of people read it. It was intensely personal and it conveyed to people what he was reading and thinking.

Dr. Campbell Morgan sent a letter of greeting on Chadwick's twenty-first anniversary congratulating him on the news.

> With all my heart I congratulate you on reaching the twenty-first anniversary of the editorship of *Joyful News* – but I congratulate *J.N.* far more on having had such editorship for so long a period – and for its sake I hope it may long have that privilege. Your work on the paper is always a delight to me. The literary style of your writing is a constant joy. I agree with the opinion expressed to me personally by Sir W. Robertson Nicoll concerning it – that it is among the finest being done in religious journalism. I value it far more for its constant loyalty to the really fundamental things of our faith. And again I thank God for the spirit of your work. It is sometimes caustic – finely so – but never vitriolic. And turning to lighter matters, I love your fairy stories ever and

anon, and the child-like which has ever enriched your writing. May you long continue.[23]

In 1893, during his third year at Wesley, Leeds, Samuel Chadwick made the first of seven trips to America. It was during the year of the Chicago Exhibition and Moody had invited him to take part in evangelistic campaign. He preached at the services, lectured to the students at the Bible Institute and was invited to Northfield. While visiting and preaching at the Indian Springs' Camp Meeting, he spoke on the place holiness has in the American-like style.

> No one is admitted to its platform who does not subscribe and testify to it as a definite experience subsequent to regeneration. The call is 'The Second Blessing.' It corresponds to our Southport Convention as it was at its beginning. They stand for the doctrine of *eradication* of inbred sin and *imparted* holiness, as against the Keswick teaching of *repression* of sin and *imputed* holiness. There is no place in the world where the doctrine has suffered so much as to America. Every form of extravagance, folly, fanaticism, and immortality has been associated with the name. The Churches have come to dread everything associated with the name of holiness. Yet the doctrine is in the Book, and we dare not be silent because some abuse. Knowing these things, I went with an open mind and much prayer that I might be able to discern and rejoice in whatever was of grace. Unfortunately they constrained me to preach three times in a day and a half, and I was deprived of hearing as much as I hoped. I heard enough, however, to give me ample basis for judgement, and for the truths I preached I am prepared to answer any time anywhere.[24]

In 1916 the South African Conference of the Methodist Church celebrated its Centenary. Chadwick was chosen to go and at the end of March set sail. The world was at war and the journey by sea was fraught with difficulties and Samuel was a week late when he walked down the gangway to set foot on South African soil. It was Good Friday and the English preacher ministered in the Metropolitan Church and there was great scenes at the altar when dozens of people sought

---

[23] Campbell Morgan, *Samuel Chadwick*, pp.138, 139.

[24] D.W. Lambert, *The Testament of Samuel Chadwick*, p.148.

the Lord. Later he was taken to Shaw Memorial Church called after William Shaw, the pioneer Methodist minister who went to South African with the early settlers in 1820. Chadwick did not have many opportunities of addressing large gatherings of natives and he enjoyed speaking through interpreters. He visited all the chief towns in the Sub-Continent, Johannesburg, Pretoria, Kimberley and Port Elizabeth. When he was at Durban, the news of Lord Kitchener's death arrived. The Governor of South Africa appointed the following Friday as a memorial day and services were everywhere at noon. Chadwick was asked if he would preach and reaching a station, he announced the hymn, 'Nearer, my God, to Thee,' and everyone knew the words. Chadwick spoke for about ten minutes and then he prayed.

Samuel Chadwick was known throughout Methodism for his preaching and his abilities. In 1902 he was elected into the Legal Hundred and in later years the Conference added further honours by sending him as one of their Delegates to the Isle of Man Synod and to the Irish Conference. In 1918, to the joy of all his brethren, he was elected to the Presidential Chair. He wrote and consulted with the leaders of the other Free Churches throughout the country and made arrangements for a great Nonconformist Thanksgiving in the Royal Albert Hall for the following Saturday. The auditorium was crowded with more than ten thousand people. For the first time in English history, the King and Queen attended a Nonconformist service. The Prince of Wales and Princess Mary were with them, and the Prime Minister, Lloyd George, also attended. Dr. Jowett conducted the service and Mr. Chadwick took the thanksgiving. The singing was glorious and the scene so impressive.

Samuel Chadwick wrote a letter to the Methodist people and reminded them of their responsibility.

> I do not tell you for whom you should vote, but how you should vote as to make it a Christian witness in the interests of the Kingdom of God. This you can do by giving heed to the character of the candidate for whom you vote, and his attitude to the principles for which the Christian witness stands.... No vote should be given to the incompetent, however godly, to a bad man, however capable.... The Christian witness stands

> for certain well-defined principles of the Kingdom of God. The Gospel of Christ is the Gospel of the Kingdom. The duty of the Church is to translate those principles into laws of life and conduct. Righteousness is the first law of the Kingdom. Sacrifice is the law of its spirit, and service is the law of its distinction.... Vote early. Vote honestly. Vote faithfully and leave the issues with God. God save the King, revive religion, prosper the nation, and bless the people.[25]

The College was again in full swing and he had to balance that with the increasing demands on his time. He went north to fulfil a promise to conduct a United Evangelistic Mission in Edinburgh. The people gathered and gave him an enthusiastic reception. Evan Roberts, the famous Welsh evangelist, sent him the following message, 'May the "big venture of faith" be a great success. May the Missioner be always confident; the message throughout the period accurate and effective; and the whole mission a beautiful blend of virtuous colours – clothed in the beauty of holiness.'[26] On the first Sunday Chadwick preached at Free St. George's. The mission services were held in Free Church Assembly Hall with seats for two thousand people. Crowds gathered and Chadwick wrote of people confessing their faith in Christ and many people have found a crisis and a Pentecost.

In 1922 Samuel Chadwick was elected President of the Free Church Council. The Assembly over which he presided was in Liverpool and there was about two thousand people; he charged them that this was going to be a year of blessing and he was looking for a thousand converted. Civic authorities recognised the influence of Free Churches when they all come together and Newcastle-on-Tyne was chosen to hold the service in Brunswick Wesley Chapel. Chadwick was invited to the service with the Mayor and Corporation and all public services were gathered. Chadwick preached and he mentioned that only now and then did he preach to such a gathering of influential and representative men. During the year Chadwick commented that there

---

25 D.W. Lambert, *The Testament of Samuel Chadwick*, pp.185, 186.

26 Evan Roberts, *Samuel Chadwick*, p.209.

was a large proportion of churches that received a baptism of fire and it was a year of blessing that he enjoyed.

Chadwick had no sooner laid down the reins of his office than he was planning a building at Cliff. Starting in 1919 the College had been crowded to capacity and men shared bedrooms in order to accommodate the crowds. The task of raising ten thousand pounds was needful but all at Cliff were confident that Samuel Chadwick was in touch with the Lord and all would be free of debt. It was in the plans to open a new Library on the ground floor with an additional twenty-five bedrooms overhead. Chadwick laid the first sod on July 26, 1923, and it was a great day for Samuel Chadwick when all the debts were paid.

James Gordon sums up the personal appearances as Chadwick had the power and influences for so many years.

> During his time as editor of *Joyful News* the paper developed as an organ devoted to encouraging on the one hand an intensive and experiential personal piety, and on the other a stringent social criticism which was sometimes enlightened but not infrequently simplistic. Over a period of several years, for example, the paper commented on housing conditions, the plight of starving Russian refugees, the basis of a just peace following the armistice, the Irish question, miners' strikes, educational policy, sabbath observance, temperance, debt and gambling. On some occasions Chadwick spoke with weight and experience, forging powerful arguments from a Christian moral perceptive. Nevertheless the moral vigilance, spiritual warmth, and straightforward language of *Joyful News* made it an effective medium for Chadwick's distinctive emphases. Chadwick's style was tailor-made for a popular paper. He was a life time student of words. He told his students he had read slowly Chambers dictionary four times. Short sentences, strong verbs of action, contrasting clauses, a feel for the fright word and a preacher's preference for the imperative mood make for working lively and vigorous.[27]

There was no part of Cliff that gave Mr. Chadwick more joy than his Bible Schools. It began in 1905 and now August was given over to the

---

[27] James Gordon, *Evangelical Spirituality*, pp.256, 257.

lecturers and crowds gathered each year to share in them. The Principal was fortunate in those he choose as lecturers and the list reads like an advertisement. The visiting lecturers have included men of the calibre of Campbell Morgan, Revd. W.L. Watkinson, Professor Richard Moulton, Dr. James Orr, Bishop Hughes, Dr. James Moulton, Revd. F. Luke Wiseman, Dr. Waddy Moss, and the Revd. Dinsdale Young. From the beginning the Summer Schools have been crowded and this without any advertisement. The four weeks was by no means a holiday. The rising bell went at six in the morning and at seven a preaching service was conducted in the Chapel. From nine-thirty to twelve-thirty there were Bible Lectures and at night to foreign missions, evangelism and hymnology, and one night to the Methodist doctrine of entire sanctification. There was always strong meat and plenty of it. The common factor was that they were all Local Preachers in the Methodist Church. They was mostly of a lack of education but the questions asked at the close of lectures showed that the men were not indifferent to modern speculation and modern terminology.

As the 1920's closed it was becoming evident that all was not well with Samuel Chadwick. This gave rise to serious consideration and on two occasions when in the middle of a speech, Chadwick's mind became blank and he struggled to explain himself. He went into Sheffield Hospital in 1927 and he struggled manfully to carry on his work. When a second operation was necessary in 1930, Chadwick himself knew it was the end. Frequently it was necessary for him to go to bed and he had to curtail his work, and give out that he would accept no more. He went on with his work and continued writing *Joyful News*. The periods he spent in bed were always periods of reflection, of vision and of commission. He christened these periods 'Sleepy Hollow' but he was assured that he would not go till everything he had seen would be accomplished.

The Trek Movement of Evangelistic Friars was born while he was recuperating. Thomas Champness had his *Joyful News* evangelists, Thomas Cook his Gospel cars, and the name of Samuel Chadwick will always be associated with Cliff College Trekkers who have taken the

Gospel to every corner of the land. In the summer of 1925 the first Trek set out. All the way they preached and testified and everywhere they saw men and women converted to God. They became known as the Methodist Friars and combined the universal gospel and assured testimony of the early Methodists. They have borne witness on village greens and market squares, on crowded beaches and the race-courses, to crowds of every size and kind. Everywhere they found a ready response to their appeal. Before Samuel Chadwick died his Trekkers were known all over the country. There were few Methodist circuits in which they had not borne witness, and wherever they went their success in leading men and women to God was the joy of the Principal's heart. At the close of their summer's work, they would return to Cliff College and tell Samuel Chadwick their story with tears in his eyes.

In February 1931 Chadwick went to Oxford Place, Leeds, for the last time. Ever since he had left he had returned year by year for the Anniversary Sunday. On this occasion he preached at night from the text, 'I have fought a good fight, I have finished my course, I have kept the faith' (2 Tim. 4:7). He commenced his sermon by announcing that this was not to be his 'Swan Song,' but on Monday he was sure in his heart that he would never see Oxford Place again. He entered into building plans again, improving the College Entrance Halls and publishing his much-beloved book, *The Path of Prayer*. Apart from *Humanity and God,* which he published in 1903, his only other book was, *The Path of Prayer*. All his life was spent in writing and it is surprising that only two books were published. There are about twelve other books on Samuel Chadwick but they have come from his writing and they will be looked at presently.

Bearing the date, August 21, 1931, and dedicated to his wife, there are sixteen chapters to this book. The chapters all appeared in *Joyful News* and they have now appeared as a book.

> They were not written for critics nor for scholars, but for plain people who are deeply religious and sincerely simple in their trust. Hundreds of these readers wrote me grateful letters, and begged me that the articles should be put into a book. They are sent forth in the form in which it

> pleased God to bless them. No one can be more conscious of their limitations than myself. Of one thing I am confident; I have written out of an honest heart, that has sought above all things to be effectual in the communion and ministry of Prayer, and to which there has come no greater joy than the fellowship of the inner sanctuary. For more than fifty years I have read in every school of Prayer, and especially in the devotional literature of the Mystics and the Discipline Orders; but I have written out of the experience of my own prayer life, in the hope that what has helped me may be helpful to others.[28]

Chapter one begins 'The Sign of Prayer,' and God and man are inseparable. Belief in God and belief in prayer are elemental and intuitive. The teaching of the Old Testament is full of the subject of prayer. All the crises in the life of the Lord were linked with special seasons of prayer, though He never sought to explain its mystery.

> God speaks of prayer in terms of wonder: 'Behold, he prayeth' (Acts 9, 11). This is how God speaks and to Him there is nothing more glorious than prayer. It would seem as if the biggest thing in God's universe is a man who prays. Behold! In that word there is wonder, rapture, exultation. In the estimate of God prayer is more wonderful than all the wonders of the heavens, more glorious than all the mysteries of the earth, more mighty than all the forces of creation.... That is a conversion that was the result of an experience. What was the experience? Paul says that in the experience it pleased God to reveal His Son in him. When God speaks of it He sums it all up in the words, 'Behold, he prayeth.'[29]

In the second part of prayer, 'Learning to Pray,' Chadwick says it is not other people's prayer that makes men and women pray. All true prayer, the prayer that prevails, is personal, intimate, and original. The secret of Elijah's power in prayer was that he prayed in his prayer. He prayed with prayer; he prayed in his prayer. He did not say prayer; he prayed in praying. His whole personality was in his supplication. It is the prayer that prevails. Formal routine of temple-service and the regular reading of second-hand inspiration and no understanding are neither acceptable to God nor profitable to man. There is no way to learn to

---

[28] Samuel Chadwick, 'Foreword,' *The Path of Prayer*, 1931, pp.v, vi.

[29] Samuel Chadwick, *The Path of Prayer*, pp.11, 12.

pray but by praying. No reasoned philosophy of prayer ever taught a soul to pray. The subject is beset with problems, but there are no problems of prayer to the man who prays. There have been men and women that were mighty in prayer, and they learned to pray. There was a period in their lives when they were as others in the matter of prayer, but they became mighty with God and prevailed. In every instance there was a crisis of grace, but it was in the discipline of grace that they discovered the secret of prayer. Such a life of prayer costs time. Learners give hours regularly every day that they may become proficient in art and mechanism. Our Lord rose before daybreak that He might pray, and not infrequently He spent all night in prayer. All praying saints have spent hours every day in prayer. It ought to be possible to give God one hour out of twenty-four all to Himself. Let us make a start in the discipline of training in prayer by setting apart a fixed time every day for the exercise of prayer.

In Chapter 4 of his book, Chadwick comes to 'The Inner Room and the Closed Door,' (Matt. 6: 5, 6). He begins by telling us how it was with him and the reasons he was successful.

> I want to write quite frankly, and in the first person. All my life I have wanted to learn to pray. In my zeal I have experimented and explored in likely and unlikely ways and schools of prayer, and without pose or pride I want in meekness and humility to tell you what I have learned. I speak for myself. I judge no man's method, criticise no man's counsel, challenge no man's experience. I speak with utmost simplicity, and you must judge what I say. Let us begin with the difficulty of privacy. There are tens of thousands of Christ's disciples who have no room to which they can retire for private prayer. They live with other people, sleep with other people, work with other people. They cannot escape from people. Is not this a reason why the door of the House of God should never be closed?.... Attention is an act of the will. By patience the soul is won, and by discipline the mind is trained. God is in secret. Let the first act be to affirm the fact of the Holy Presence. Call every faculty of mind and body to remembrance, recognition, and realisation of the God that heareth in secret and seeth in secret. Hold the mind to this fact. Tolerate no distraction, allow no diversions, indulge no dissipation. Every faculty must be alert. Dreaming is not meditation. Dozing is not thinking.

Moping is not praying. Prayer in the secret place demands every faculty at its best.[30]

Chadwick says that with him there is only the Bible and he seeks no aids to devotion such as the Cross or Crucifix. Questions of criticism, textual or otherwise, does not enter his mind, and its promises, meditations, call to worship and prayers are enough for him. The word of God is more to him than food and it thrills and moves him with tremendous power. It is in those times that God speaks and nothing should be allowed while God is talking to the soul. There, in that place, one can talk to God about other people; the family, the Church, the business, the friendships, the state of the world are all the subjects of earnest and believing private prayer. The God in secret is our Father and prayer is filial; we talk as sons and daughters in the Father's House. It is in the secret place that we learn that silence is the best speech and listening is the best part of praying. Those who speak are heard, and those who listen hear. Of Jesus it is said: 'And in the morning, a great while before day, He rose up and went out, and departed into a desert place, and there prayed' (Mark 1:35).

In chapter six of his book, Samuel Chadwick speaks on 'Praying in the Name.' The most incredible things are promised in prayer. Nothing was too hard for the Lord and nothing was impossible to those who prayed. There is no limit to the possibility of prayer, and the Old Testament confirms and attests the promises by examples and demonstrating of its power. The promises to prayer reaches its climax in the Upper Room on that memorable night of revelation and tragedy. He declared Himself to be the basis of prayer. They were to pray in His Name, and they would be heard for His sake. What extraordinary promises are pledged to prayer in the Name of our Lord and Saviour Jesus Christ (John 14:17). They abound in universal and unconditional terms. They are all things whatsoever are asked. Prayer reaches its highest level when offered in the Name which is above every name, for it lifts the petitioner into unity and identity with Himself. Our Lord never explained what was meant by praying in His Name. God was in

---

[30] Samuel Chadwick, *The Path of Prayer*, pp.32, 33.

His Name. He had made them an elect people, that they might be the interpreters, custodians, and witnesses of His Name.

Such correspondence and identification with Christ secures the balance and identification of the promises given to prayer. God was found of men when they cried unto Him out of a great need; when they sought Him with all their heart, and when there was sincerity of purpose and motive. In the prayer in the Name all conditions are unified and simplified in Him. Sincerity is tested in the Name. Motive is judged in the Name. Prayer is proved in the Name. Prayer is sanctified in the Name. Prayer offered in the Name of Christ are scrutinised and sanctified by His nature, His purpose, and His will.

> We are heard for His sake. He is the petitioner. He ever liveth to make intercession for us. In the Apocalypse He is represented as taking our prayers and adding to them the fire of the Altar that makes them prevail. He told His disciples He was going to the Father, and that He was going to pray on their behalf, and whatever they asked of the Father in His Name the Father would do it. Not for their own sake, but for His sake they would be heard. In some such way we pray in Christ's Name. He endorses our petitions and makes our prayers His own, and 'the Father hears Him pray.' We are not heard for our much speaking, nor for our loud shouting. Neither are we heard for our fine phrasing, nor our much weeping. Neither are we heard for our good works, nor for our self-denials. Prayer in His Name is heard for His Name's sake. In the secret sanctuary of the inner chamber we ask, seek, and knock in His Holy Name, and present our prayers in the sure confidence of His wonderful and glorious word: 'You did not choose Me, but I chose you, and appointed you.... that whatsoever you shall ask of the Father in My Name, He may give it you '(John 15:16).[31]

Chapter 7 in the book is entitled, 'Praying in the Spirit,' and Chadwick opens with a testimony that transformed his life.

> Early in the year 1882 there came to be an experience that lifted my life to a new plane of understanding and of power. I received the gift of the Holy Spirit. The demands of an impossible task awakened me to a sense of need. I began to pray for power for service, and God led me to the

---

[31] Samuel Chadwick, *The Path of Prayer*, pp.53, 54.

answer by way of equipment for power. It was power I wanted. I wanted power that I might succeed, and my chief concern for power was the success it would bring. I wanted success that would fill the chapel, save the people, and bring down the strong fortifications of Satan with a crash. I was young and I was in a hurry. He led me to Pentecost. The key to all my life is in that experience. It awakened my mind as well as cleansing my heart. It gave me a new joy and a new power, a new love and a new compassion. It gave me a new Bible and a new message. Above all else, it gave me a new understanding and ministry of prayer; it taught me to pray in the Spirit.[32]

The work of the Holy Spirit is always in co-operation and He never works alone. He depends upon human-operation for the medication of His mind, the manifestation of His truth, and the effectual working of His will. He indwells the Body of Christ, as Christ dwelt in the Body prepared for Him by the Holy Spirit. The Holy Spirit does nothing of Himself; His mission is to glorify Christ, and all He does is based upon the finished work of Christ. He could not be given until Jesus was glorified, and in experience there can be no Pentecost until there is a Coronation. The Spirit is the Coronation gift of Jesus, whom the Father has made to be both Lord and Spirit. Those who pray in the Spirit must be in the Spirit, and if the Spirit of God is to make intercession for us He must dwell in us. If we live after the flesh we die, but if we are led of the Spirit, then the Spirit dwells in us, lives through us, and works by us.

He instructs and inspires all true prayer. There is no truer word than that; 'We know not what we should pray for as we ought' (Rom. 8:26). We cannot see deep enough or far enough to know what is our real need. Most people would like good health, home comfort, congenial conditions, a little more money, and better success; but who can tell if these would be for their ultimate good? God sees deeper and farther, and He may will otherwise. How often have people pleaded with breaking hearts that a life might be spared living to thank God that the Lord took when He did? He knew what was coming and took them

[32] Samuel Chadwick, *The Path of Prayer*, pp.55, 56.

from the evil to come. The Holy Spirit knows the mind of Christ and the will of God, and He teaches us how to pray and what to ask for.

> The Holy Spirit creates the conditions of prayer. He sanctifies desire and directs it into the will of God, so that we desire what God wills to give. That is how it comes to pass that if we delight ourselves in the Lord, we can be sure that He will give us the desires of our heart. We want what He wills. The Spirit brings to expression the unutterable things of the soul. His groanings are before our praying, and our hearts are born of His travail. In Him is the supply of life and desire, wisdom and faith, intercession and power. He quickens desire, purifies motive, inspires confidence, and assures faith.... The Spirit within our spirit prays, working in us to will and to do the will and good pleasure of our Father which is in Heaven. The assurance of answered prayer comes from Him, and He it is that makes prayer the mightiest force in the universe of God. The secret of it all is by Him. The biggest thing God ever did for me was to teach me to pray in the Spirit.[33]

Chapter 10 is 'The Recompense of Prayer,' and Chadwick wants to share with his people the delights of prayer. It has been said that the mountains of the Bible will repay the climber, and no life is richer in mountain scenes than that of Moses. For forty years he had wandered among their solitary heights, feeding his flock and grappling with the great problems of his people and their God. It was amid the silence of the everlasting hills that he was fitted for the work of delivering and guiding the people of God. His service began and ended in the Mount. On the eve of every new development, and on every critical occasion, God called him, and he went up. Whenever the burden of his charge oppressed him, he hastened to seek God in the Mount. There is a very special sense in which God dwells in the secret place. God wants us in the Mount. Before daybreak Jesus and Moses were alone with God.

Moses found God in the mountains we are afraid to climb. He found himself and he found his vocation. He found that a stick he had carried daily was a symbol and instrument of Divine power. It was there he received the law. After forty days alone with God, he brought heaven's law to earth on two tablets of stone. Those laws remain to this day the

---

33 Samuel Chadwick, *The Path of Prayer*, pp.59-61.

foundation of all righteous government among men. After centuries of progress they are still the basis of civilisation. The way to the Mount is still open. The Divine pattern of each life is still to be seen in the secret place of the Most High God. The humblest follower of Jesus may know the Divine Will at first hand. The Divine attention to detail is amazing. Nothing is too trivial for Omniscience. When God speaks, His speech is easily understood. All questions of the plan should be settled in the Mount, and where there is certainty in the Mount there will be victory on the levels and in the valleys.

Chadwick then turns to power and the place of fellowship with God.

> There is a wonderful story in Exodus 17. It was Israel's first battle. The Amalekites came against them in Rephidim. Joshua commanded the hosts of Israel, and Moses went up into the Mount to pray. The fluctuations of the battle were astonishing. In turns the opposing hosts prevailed, until it was found that the issue of the battle was not with the fighters in the field, but with the intercessors in the Mount. It was the weapon-less hand of prayer the ruled the battle. 'And it came to pass, that Moses held up his hands, that Israel prevailed: and when he let down his hand, Amalek prevailed' (Exod. 17:11). It was the weaponless hand of prayer that ruled the battle. Is it necessary to point the moral of the tale? Power is the recompense of prayer. It takes us long to learn that power is more important than organisation, more powerful than armies, more influential than wealth, and mightier than all learning. Prevalent prayer makes men invincible. Those who prevail in the secret place of the Most High cannot be beaten anywhere. All things are possible to secret prayer.... In the Mount the Lord spoke unto Moses face to face, as a man speaks unto his friend. The inner chamber is an audience chamber where the soul enters into friendly intercourse and mutual interchange. It is a place for listening as well as for speech. The most important part of prayer is not what we say to God, but what God says to us.... Glory is the recompense of prayer.... God wants us in the Mount and He wants us in the valley. Moses died in the Mount. Those who go up and down at God's bidding are sure to end in going up to heaven to come down no more.[34]

---

[34] Samuel Chadwick, *The Path of Prayer*, pp.76-82.

Chapter 15 is called 'Praying for Divine Healing,' and Chadwick introduces a subject that has been often written and spoken about. He confesses there are times when the problem of divine healing is linked to James 5:15; 'And the prayer of faith shall save the sick, and the Lord shall raise him up.' He has searched the Scriptures from end to end that he might know the truth but the subject is full of difficulties.

> I myself have been healed through the Prayer of Faith. In my ministry I have been used of God to the healing of the sick. I have never exercised the Ministry of Healing except at the urgent request of the sick and a sure constraint of the Spirit of God. There are those for whom I would have given my right hand if I could have prayed them to health, but I have had to see them suffer and die. Some have suffered untold anguish of mind because they sought for healing in vain. This has been my problem. While I was yet a young minister, one of the workers of the Church was stricken with disease. We claimed the promises, and some of the best people I have ever known prayed earnestly and believing for his recovery. We refused to believe that faith could fail. He died while we prayed.[35]

Chadwick then gives the example of how Revd. W.H. Tindall was healed at the Southport Convention. He was stricken with a disease in his throat and he was silent about a year and he was President at the time he was ill. The specialists gave no hope of a recovery and he was a pathetic and silent figure. Prayer was offered for him continually and on the Friday morning no one could pray for anything except Mr. Tindall's voice. The prayer meeting was led by Dr. Ebenezer Jenkins and he announced: 'This is the most remarkable prayer-meeting I have ever known,' and placing his hand on Mr. Tindall's head he declared that all would hear him speak. That night Mr. Tindall spoke in the tent and was heard by twelve hundred people and he preached without loss of voice till the end of his life.

> The teaching of the Bible is for me the last word. I accept it whether I understand it or not, and the Scriptures teach that *the Lord is our healer*. That is one of the names by which He is revealed. It is also beyond dispute that our Lord and Saviour regarded healing as an integral part of His ministry. The gift of healing was, and is, among the gifts of the

---

[35] Samuel Chadwick, *The Path of Prayer*, pp.113, 114.

Spirit. Healing was part of the Apostolic Ministry. The gift has never been withdrawn from the Church. Through all the ages there have been witnesses to its power.[36]

The Bible associated sickness with Satan. Jesus attributed some sicknesses to the devil and both Luke and Acts say plainly that Satan has bound the woman eighteen years (Luke 12:16), and in Acts we read: 'Jesus went about doing good and healing the diseases of all who were oppressed of the Devil' (Acts 10:38). Sickness and sin are associated in redemption and healing. Matthew sees in divine ministry of our Lord the fulfilment of Isaiah's prophecy. 'He cast out the spirit with His word, and healed all that were sick; that it might be fulfilled which was spoken by Isaiah the prophet saying, "Himself took our infirmities, and bare our sickness"' (Matt. 7:16, 17). Paul healed others but he accepted his own sufferings as part of the afflictions of Christ. Epaphroditus was healed of the Lord (Phil. 2:27), but Trophimus he had to leave at Miletum sick (2 Tim. 4:20). Chadwick believes in divine healing.

> I believe in the healing power of faith. The grounds of my faith are in Him. I trust His Word, the redeeming work of Christ, and the sanctifying power of His Spirit. I am bound to believe that sickness may be in the will of God, for the purpose of discipline, for the glory of His grace, and the Ministry of Christ. I am sure that Divine Healing is a fact. I am sure that many people are sick who ought never to have been sick, and who might now be healed. I am sure that no life is so health-giving and so radiant as the life of joyous and obedient faith. I am sure I believe with all my heart and mind in Divine Healing, in spite of the fact that I am often ailing.[37]

Samuel Chadwick reserves the 'The Problem of Unanswered Prayer' to his last chapter. He has prayed all his life but there are problems in unanswered prayer. Now, a few years before he dies, he returns to spell out the problems and difficulties of unanswered prayer.

> It is many years since I first wrote on Unanswered Prayer. The problem became acute when the man for whom we were praying so earnestly and

---

[36] Samuel Chadwick, *The Path of Prayer*, pp.117, 118.

[37] Samuel Chadwick, *The Path of Prayer*, p.120.

> confidently dies while we prayed. The shock of it was overwhelming. It had never occurred to us that he might die. We had claimed the promise. We were absolutely sure of the Word. I do not think my faith was ever so tried. We went back to the Word, and God gave me a message that has brought consolation to many, and through all the years it has been a stronghold for my trust. Many years have passed since then, but the truth abides, and though it may involve some repetition, I want to pass the message to others.[38]

There can be little doubt that God answers prayer. All men and women are commanded to pray, at all times, in all places and for all needs. Assurances are given that God answers prayer. The promises are explicit and the Scriptures are full of examples and encouragement. Everything that concerns man is of interest to God and is a proper subject for prayer. God does not divide our needs into sacred and secular, spiritual and material. When Samuel Chadwick was puzzled about prayer, God took him and showed him three examples of unanswered prayer.

The first one is Moses (Deut. 3:23-35), where Moses prayed that he might go over into Canaan. Moses had performed all that God said to him but when they came to the desert of Zion, the people murmured against God (Num. 20:3). God intervened and told Moses and Aaron to take his rod and speak before the rock, 'and thou shalt bring forth to them water out of the rock' (Num. 20:8). Moses and Aaron went to the rock but instead of commanding the rock, 'Moses lifted up his hand, and with his rod he smote the rock twice: and the water came out abundantly.' God was angry with Moses and in v.12 we read: 'And the Lord spoke unto Moses and Aaron, "Because ye believed me not, to sanctify me in the eyes of the children of Israel, therefore ye shall not bring this congregation into the land which I have given them."' Just as the unbelief of the nation prevented them from entering the Promised Land, so Moses' rebellion barred him from this privilege. Now when the promised land was lying before them, Moses prayed that he would go over into Canaan, the Lord rejected him and he died

---

38 Samuel Chadwick, *The Path of Prayer*, p.121.

on the slopes of Moab. Because of sin he was not privileged to go in and enjoy the land.

Chadwick then turned to Elijah's prayer as recorded in the book of 1 Kings 19:4: 'O Lord, take away my life; for I am not better than my fathers.' After his triumph at Carmel and the end of the prophets of Baal in verse 40, Elijah returned to Jezreel and Jezebel spoke of him saying: 'So let the gods do to me, and more also, if I make not thy life as the life of one of them by tomorrow about this time' (19:2). Elijah felt frightened and he ran away and sat down under a juniper tree and pleaded with God to end his life. But God had other plans for Elijah, much bigger than death, and he went up to heaven in a chariot of fire. Chadwick argues that this plan was more wonderful than death and apart from the Lord, he was the only one transported into glory.

Chadwick's third example is taken from 2 Cor. 12:7-9, where Paul prays for the removal of affliction. The great apostle was beset with 'a thorn in the flesh,' and he prayed that it might be lifted. Three times he sought the Lord to remove his thorn but it was to remain with him all his life. All his ministry he was bothered by Satan 'lest I should be exalted above measure,' (v.7), but the prayer was not answered. 'These men occupy a prominent place in Scripture, and yet each was denied his request. Their prayers are fairly representative, and cover the ground of the problem.'[39]

None of these prayers was unanswered. They were not granted, but they were answered and 'No' was the answer. When a request is refused, it is as truly answered as when it is granted. Refusal may be the only answer possible to love and wisdom and truth. The Lord knows the future as well as the past. The immediate may imperil the future. The eagerness for a mess of pottage may involve the loss of an inheritance. God spared Hezekiah fifteen years, but he had better have done when the Lord sent for him.

> Delays are not denials, and it pays to wait God's time. Moses got into Canaan, and Elijah went to heaven by a more glorious way than that of

---

[39] Samuel Chadwick, *The Path of Prayer*, p.123.

a juniper tree. No inspired prayer of faith is ever refused.... He took Elijah to heaven by a much more wonderful way than that of the grave. Paul never had any use for juniper trees, and to him God said, 'My grace is sufficient for thee' (2 Cor. 12:9). In the experience that first sorely tried our faith, God sent help out of the darkness. Through the tears of a broken heart the vision came, and when the memorial card was sent it bore this text, which rebuked our unbelief, 'He asked life of Thee, and Thou gavest it him, even length of days for ever and ever' (Ps. 21:4). So in glory shall we find our prayers have been interpreted according to the infinite wisdom and eternal love of God our Father.

The last time he addressed Conference was in Birmingham in 1931. The July Committee had recommended, as a candidate for the ministry, a young man from the East End Mission. Ministers had spoken on this candidate to as his ability in seeking and saving the lost. Samuel Chadwick rose in his place and his words were a plea not to deal harshly with the young man. He gloried in the ministry of this man and said that he was at the end of his peace and pleaded for what the young man had done. The Conference overruled the Committee and voted for his acceptance.

The year was filled with Presidential addresses and Chadwick looked forward to visiting the Irish Conference as well as the churches of the Methodists in Wales. Every place visited by Chadwick reaped revivals and great harvest of souls. However, there was one place he looked forward to visiting and this was his own church at Burnley and a great reception was planned in his honour. The folk who knew him turned up in scores and Methodist people in the area made speeches. Burnley was hailing one of its greatest sons that afternoon and Chadwick told later of those addresses that hailed him as the lad who had grown up the Wesley Church in Burnley. He told that during the interval for tea, many people came up to him and said: 'Aye, Sam lad, who'd ha' thought it?'

The consent of the will lay at the heart of Chadwick's own second experience. He called it 'a crisis of obedience' and claimed it gave him the key to all his thinking, all his service and all his life. 'There came into my soul a deep peace, a thrilling joy and a sense of

> power.'[40] Just as the original Pentecost had brought illumination of mind, assurance of heart, intensity of love, fullness of power and exuberance of joy, so the believer's personal Pentecost carries an equally potent spiritual payload. Chadwick made bold claims for this second experience of grace. The experience of prayer is decisively changed because before Pentecost we pray in the Spirit, after Pentecost the Spirit prays through us. In describing the overall benefits of what he calls the Baptism of the Holy Spirit, he uses absolute terms with total confidence. 'All fullness of life, all resources of vitality, all certainty in prayer, all certitude of glory – all and everything is in the dwelling Presence and Power of the Holy Spirit of God in Christ Jesus our Lord.'[41] That last complex clause contains the key elements of Chadwick's spiritual thought.[42]

On Wednesday, October 8, 1919, the College re-opened and Samuel was now in his sixtieth year and was at the height of his powers. Speaking of those years in particular, Samuel Chadwick was adamant that the life of Cliff had no meaning except it was evangelistic.

> Our faith is the faith of an evangelist, and our theology is the Gospel of Grace. Evangelistic work must be based upon evangelistic truth: we believe and teach the Word of God as the divinely-inspired and final authority in all matters of faith and conduct. It is the revelation of the Divine Mind and the inspired record of Redeeming Grace – progressive, infallible, universal.... The Spirit that inspired the Word keeps it living and active and we teach the Bible intelligently, systematically, reverently.... We preach Jesus Christ both Saviour and Lord. Salvation is the universal need, and Christ alone is the universal Saviour. The Gospel is for every man, for Christ died for all, and is able to save to the uttermost every one that comes to God by Him. The College stands frankly for the definite experience of Full Salvation. Thomas Cook was one of the most sanest teachers and witnesses to the doctrine and he was a radiant saint of God. The College stands for the same testimony. This is the one essential element in the equipment of an evangelist. Evangelistic efficiency finds its effectiveness in Pentecostal power. This is the Methodist witness, and in Christ there is a fullness of grace for a holy life and of power that prevails with men.... We have no mechanical

---

[40] Samuel Chadwick, *The Way to Pentecost*, p.32.

[41] Samuel Chadwick, *The Way to Pentecost*, p.36.

[42] James Gordon, *Evangelical Spirituality*, p.261, 1991.

> tests of experience. We coerce no man's faith. We compel no man's will. Cliff College stands explicitly for a Saviour who is able to save all men with an uttermost salvation.[43]

In the early days Chadwick had his Anniversary on Easter Monday at Sheffield but it was felt that Methodists would like to come to Cliff and from 1921, they were transferred to the College. Each Whit-Monday would see more and more Methodists gather and a tent was erected in the park. Chadwick made the Cliff College Anniversary the largest in the Methodist year. The railway companies ran special trains to bring large contingents from London, Bristol, Manchester and Sunderland and for once a year, the quiet Derbyshire Dale was seething with people. The offering plates were full of money and at the close of Whit-Monday, the money they raised was four thousand pounds, a huge sum for the 1920's. Chadwick preached in the tent on the opening Sunday and for years he would turn again to the first four verses of Acts chapter 2, and many people said that this was the finest sermon they had heard. The people loved coming and Samuel was overjoyed to see his friends again. No one who was present for the 1932 celebrations will ever forget the last time Samuel Chadwick preached. He had been ill for months but with Whit-Monday approaching, he was gathering strength and preached one of the mightiest sermons he had preached. As the meeting went on, Samuel returned indoors and watched from a bedroom window. The offering for the Whit-Sunday service was nearly four thousand pounds and Mr. Chadwick appeared on the platform. The people had no idea that this was to be his last. In two or three sentences he told them that this was his last. The huge throng was silent. He called all who love him to a new and complete consecration. Ten thousand hands were lifted up and they sang it so spontaneously:

> Lord, in the strength of grace
> With a glad heart and free
> Myself, my residue of days
> I consecrate to Thee.
> Thy ransomed servant, I

[43] Samuel Chadwick, *The Testament of Samuel Chadwick*, pp.39, 40.

Restore to Thee Thy own
And, from this moment, live or die
To serve my God alone.[44]

Not a person who lived through that minute could ever forget that it was one of Charles Wesley's greatest triumphs that they said goodbye to one of Methodism's greatest preachers.

The last three years of his life were spent in 'Sleepy Hollow,' and Chadwick gives a definition of that name.

> Sleepy Hollow has often been to me a place of vision, voices, and vocation. It was in sickness that there came the call of God to the work of the ministry while I was yet a lad in obscure poverty. Nothing seemed less likely, but I cherished the vision and the call till God set before me an open door. On another occasion, an Angel of the Lord found me baffled, beaten, and bruised, after my first encounter with the kingdom of darkness; and it was he who instructed me in the way of the Lord and showed me my way about in the Scriptures.... Every Monday morning I read the forty-first chapter of Isaiah, and rejoice afresh that God gives the greatest of His promises to the weakest of His creatures.... Three years ago I lay deep in the valley of shadows. The gates of death were not far away. I have never had a serious illness in which there has not come a vision, and they have all come to pass. Sometimes it has taken many years, and often there have been long stretches that seemed far remote from the place where God has spoken; but sooner or later, the vision has come down out of heaven to earth. God showed me the unreached world and the unreached Church. I saw how from time to time God has need of adventurers, who would leave the ruts of Church organisations and ordinances and go out to preach the Gospel to the unreached everywhere, untrammelled by machinery, uninfluenced by schedules, and unhindered by entanglements. He asked me for men. I pleaded that my work seemed to be done, but He assured me that if I would live, this should be done. It is coming to pass. Not as quickly as I would like, but I can see in the dark. The first hundred pounds has been given anonymously, and the first of the Hundred Friars is at work. We shall need a Hostel and we have the site.[45]

---

44 Charles Wesley, *The Poetical Works of John and Charles Wesley*, Vol. 9, p.203.
45 Norman Dunning, *Samuel Chadwick*, pp.232-234.

At Christmas it seemed that the end had come, but he rallied again, preached at Whitsun, attended the Southport Convention and conducted his Summer Schools. The year 1932 was wearing on and early in September he was in Sleepy Hollow again and this time there was no way out. The new term was the first day of October and the Principal was able to direct affairs from his bedroom. In his last conscious moments he called his colleagues to his bedside and gave them a parting message.

> Stand together for the Word of God, but not in any stupid sense. Stand in a spirit of unity, of faith, of doctrine, according to the fourth chapter of the Ephesians. This will be the great consummation of my work and of my hopes. I have stood true to the last. I have had no doubts. I have been sure of the Living God. He knows my limitations, but I have loved Him and trusted in His mercy. My ministry has been the message of the Cross. I am not dead yet, although it seems as though the end is not far away. God is very, very good to me; and if my day's march is over, I am ready for the 'Roll-Call' in the morning.[46]

It was Saturday and those round his bed knew that his time had come. He lingered through the night and after six o'clock the struggle ceased and Samuel Chadwick was gone. His day's march was over and at daybreak on Sunday, October 16, he obeyed the summons and he passed over and on the other side the angels sounded their trumpets.

The College Chapel was a paradise of flowers and the morning service was arranged for the staff, personal friends, the students, tenants, workmen and servants about the place. All his friends were there and they had worked for him. It was a service never to be forgotten for its deep sense of the communion of saints. Ministers representative of every generation of Cliff men and of the ministry in general, were there. In some respects it was a festival of old-fashioned Methodism and no soul was unblest. The service was conducted from the terrace where he stood to conduct the last Whit-Monday evening service. The Revd. F.L. Wiseman, J.G. Freeman, J.A. Broadbelt, N.G. Dunning, J. Brice, and D.W. Lambert took part. Mr. Wiseman paid tribute to

---

[46] D.W. Lambert, *The Testament of Samuel Chadwick*, p.101.

Samuel Chadwick, 'the greatest Methodist of his time.' He was known far and wide as a mighty evangelist, a great thinker and expositor, a champion of the dispossessed, a fine saint and hero of the Kingdom of Grace.

Old Cliff men bore him to his grave. A great procession marched from the College to the Churchyard nearby and he is buried close to Thomas Cook, his great friend and predecessor. Round the grave they sang the hymn which Samuel Chadwick has used in his lectures.

Break Thou the bread of life
O Lord, to me
As Thou didst break the loaves
Beside the sea.
Beyond the sacred page
I seek Thee, Lord,
My spirit pants for Thee
O living Word![47]

Samuel Chadwick was the best known name in Methodism. He had kept the crowd while he was in Leeds and the numbers coming to his Whit-Monday gathering at Cliff College was the largest ever seen in Methodism. He was a preacher without par within Methodism and outside he was known the length and breadth of the land. After forty-two years in the ministry he was known everywhere and no one could better him in the ministry. But above all, Samuel Chadwick was a radiant Christian and wherever he went he preached the full gospel and did not fear of the people. He served them with unstinting devotion and the Methodist Friars came into being because Chadwick knew that in many areas the Gospel was not being preached. He has gone into heaven eighty-five years ago and God's people will thank the Lord for every remembrance of his life and ministry.

At the close of his book, *The Testament of Samuel Chadwick 1860-1932,* D.W. Lambert adds a personal note.

---

[47] Mary Lathbury, *The Methodist Hymn-Book*, 1904, pp.101, 102.

We remember his last words, 'I will be ready for the Roll Call in the morning.' He has gone to salute the morning, and all the trumpets are sounding for him on the other side.... Through our tears we see much and we realise some of the deeper and more precious treasures of the life that is no longer with us.... Others will speak of our leader as preacher, as evangelist, as Bible expositor, as writer and editor, in each of which excelled and will be remembered....We have sought to note that it was the life which is hidden with Christ in God. Beneath all that we loved in the man himself, the little human touches, the great heart of tenderness, the ordered life of discipline and the unfailing attitude of trust in God – below all these there was a life lived beneath the shadow of the Cross, a life of unbroken communion and unclouded fellowship, and that life goes on, and therein we rejoice and give thanks.[48]

There are three books all bearing the name of Samuel Chadwick but he never saw them in print. They are; *The Way To Pentecost* (1932); *The Call to Christian Perfection* (1943); *Through the Year with Samuel Chadwick* (1960). While Chadwick never knew what was in these books, the writings of Samuel Chadwick were used after he was dead. The opening book is called, *The Way to Pentecost,* and from its Foreword, Frederick Wiseman has written explaining the book.

> While they were still in the press, the author passed on to his great reward. The book may, therefore, be regarded as in some way a memorial volume. Throughout his ministry Mr. Chadwick has given exceptional prominence to the doctrine of the Holy Spirit: the Lord and Giver of Life, both to the Church which is Christ's body and to every member of that body.... It is not a formal treatise at all, but a selection from articles on the subject which appeared from time to time in *Joyful News*. Mr. Chadwick was not even responsible for the selection which has been made by Rev. J.I. Brice, his son in the gospel. The editor has shown much judgement in his task and has succeeded in giving a book with more than a mere appearance of unity. It has the characteristic mark of the author, full and accurate knowledge of the Scriptures, clearness of teaching, precision of statement, depth of insight and practical

[48] D.W. Lambert, *The Testament of Samuel Chadwick 1860-1932*, pp.102-105.

> purpose. It cannot fail to improve the mind, quicken the conscience and kindle desire to receive the gift of the Spirit in its fullness.[49]

The book opens with the statement: Do we believe in the Holy Ghost? The Apostles' Creed contains ten articles on the Person and Work of Christ, and only one on the Holy Spirit. No other religion has anything corresponding to the Christian doctrine of the Spirit. The Holy Scriptures declare Him to be the revealer of truth, the active agent in all works of redemption, and from first to last the instrument of Grace in the experience of salvation. In Him, and through Him, and by Him, is the power that saves. Illumination and Conviction, Repentance and Regeneration, Assurance and Sanctification, are all the work of God the eternal Spirit. The blunders of the Church are largely, if not entirely, accounted for by the neglect of the Spirit's ministry and mission. Our Lord spoke of the Spirit as the Spirit of Truth and promised that He would guide His people into all truth. Revealed truth can only be known the Revealer. The Christian religion begins in a New Birth in the power of the Spirit. It is developed under His guidance and sustained by His presence, but ignoring the Spirit, it becomes a matter of education and evolution. The Church is the body of Christ begotten, unified, and indwelt by the Spirit. The Christian religion is hopeless without the Holy Ghost.

Samuel Chadwick speaks out on the doctrine without experience.

> The Church still has a theology of the Holy Ghost but it has no living consciousness of His presence and power. Theology without experience is like faith without works: it is dead. Prayer-meetings have died out because men did not believe in the Holy Ghost. The liberty of prophesying has gone because men believe in investigation and not in inspiration. There is a dearth of conversions because faith about the New Birth as a creative act of the Holy Spirit has lost its grip on intellect and heart.... Confusion and impotence are the inevitable results when the wisdom and resources of the world are substituted for the presence and power of the Spirit.... The remedy for them is not in reproach and bitterness, but in floods and rivers, winds and sun. The answer is in the

---

[49] Fredrick Wiseman, 'Foreword,' *The Way to Pentecost*, 1931, pp.7, 8.

> demonstration of a supernatural religion, and the only way to a supernatural religion is in the abiding presence of the Spirit of God.[50]

The presence of the Spirit is vital and central to the work of the Church. Nothing else avails. The Church is called to be a 'spiritual house' and a holy priesthood. Scholarship is powerless if it is not a demonstration of His power. Prayer is vain unless He energises. When the Church is run on the same lines as a circus, there may be crowds but there is no Shekinah. That is why prayer is the test of faith and the secret of power. Miracles are the direct work of His power, and without miracles the Church cannot live. The carnal can argue but it is the Spirit that convicts. Education can civilise but is is the Spirit that convicts. The energy of the flesh can run bazaars, organise amusements and raise millions; but it is the presence of the Holy Spirit that makes a Temple of the Living God. The root-trouble of the present distress is that the Church has more faith in the world and the flesh than in the Holy Ghost, and things will get no better till we get back to His realised presence and power. The breath of the four winds would turn death into life and dry bones into mighty armies, but it only comes by prayer.

> Pentecost transforms the preacher. The commonest bush ablaze with the presence of God becomes a miracle of glory. The ministry energised by the Holy Ghost is marked by aggressive evangelism, social revolution and persecution. Holy Ghost preaching led to the burning of the books of the magic art, and it stirred up the opposition of those who trafficked in the ruin of the people. Indifference to religion is impossible where the preacher is a flame of fire. To the Church, Pentecost brought light, power, joy. No one needed to ask if they had received the Holy Ghost. Fire is self-evident. So is power. Second-hand gospels work no miracles. The only power that is adequate for Christian life and ministry work is the power of the Holy Ghost. The work of God is not by might of man or by the power of men, but by His Spirit. It is by Him the truth convicts and converts, sanctifies and saves. Our wants are many and our faults innumerable, but they are comprehended by our lack of the Holy Spirit. We want nothing but the fire. In the fullness of the Spirit there is

---

[50] Samuel Chadwick, *The Way to Pentecost*, 1932, pp.12, 13.

abundance of wisdom, resources and power. Suppose we try Pentecost![51]

Chapter 4 of his book, *The Way to Pentecost,* is entitled 'Pentecost,' and Chadwick gives an account of the Spirit in the Old Testament. There was something that began a new era for the world, a new power of righteousness, a new mission of redemption, and a new basis of fellowship. The Spirit of God has been active in the world from the beginning. He brooded upon the face of the waters when the earth was without form and void, and the order of creation was the result of His brooding. In the Old Testament He is the creative Agent, Sustainer and Renewer of the world of Nature. It was God's gift of His Spirit to man in creation that distinguished man from the rest of His works. It is a figure of speech to illustrate the fact that God communicated to man the life which was within Himself. God breathed into man His Spirit and man became a living soul. All through the Old Testament the Holy Spirit is creative, directive, energising. He came upon Moses, Bezaleel, Samson, Gideon, Samuel; and all the Prophets spake by Him. The manifestations are occasional and special. There is in them a consciousness of limitation and incompleteness, and prophets like Isaiah and Joel foretold a day of fullness of the Spirit which would be the crowning gift of redeeming grace. In the New Testament the Spirit of God is the active Agent in salvation, but in the Gospels He was 'not given' and our Lord Himself was straitened until His baptism was accomplished and He had 'sent fire upon the earth' (Luke 12:49). The Spirit was in the world but not yet given.

> At Pentecost the Holy Spirit came as He had never come before. The signs were not new except in their combination and intensity. The Wind and the Fire and the Tongues had all been associated with the gift of the Spirit, but they were now intensified, enlarged and distributed to a community of believers.... He came to fulfil the mission for which Christ came into the world. He is our Lord's Paraclete, His Advocate, and Administrator. His ministry is redemptive and regenerative. In Him the Risen and Ascended Lord finds His enlarged opportunity. He is exalted far above all rule, and authority, and dominion, and power, and to Him are given all authority in heaven and on earth, and the fullness of 'Him

[51] Samuel Chadwick, *The Way to Pentecost*, pp.17, 18.

> that filleth all in all' (Eph. 1:23).... The gift of the Spirit is inseparable from the work of the Son. The Scriptures are reticent about the Holy Spirit, but they do make it clear that the Spirit is the crowning gift of redemption through Jesus Christ, and the Spirit was through it all. As the Son learned and thereby entered into the Priesthood of Grace, so the Spirit was prepared to be His Paraclete in the Church and the world. In the fullness of time God sent forth His Son, and when the Day of Pentecost was fully come, 'they were altogether in one place' (Acts 2:1).[52]

The change in the Apostles was more wonderful than any of the marvellous portents of the day. The wind and the fire passed, but the transformation remained. The Executant of the Kingdom had come in power, and each found himself under authority and speaking as the Spirit gave him utterance. They no longer spoke with bated breath. They proclaimed the truth concerning Jesus in the open street of the city where Jesus had been murdered and a new power was at work. When the Spirit was come He would convict of sin, and righteousness and judgement, and multitudes of souls were smitten and three thousand souls cried for mercy. It was indeed 'a great and notable day' and the world has never seen such a day. Neither has Satan and his hosts of spiritual darkness ever seen such a day. The vital thing that happened at Pentecost is that the Spirit of Jesus came to abide in the hearts of men in the power of God..... What did Pentecost do for men? It brought a new dynamic of righteousness. He convicts the world of sin, of righteousness, and of judgement. Pentecost brought a new fellowship. The Kingdom of God henceforth is a new theocracy, permeated, dominated, sanctified in the Spirit of Pentecost. The new thing is not in the wind and fire, or the gift of tongues, but in the possession of the Spirit by each for the good of all. That which happened at Pentecost is the biggest thing that ever happened. And now the biggest question of all is, has it happened to us? 'Have you received the Holy Ghost?' (Acts 8:15).

---

52 Samuel Chadwick, *The Way to Pentecost*, p.25.

Samuel Chadwick now turns to 'The Pentecostal Life,' and he starts by showing what it was that came into his life.

> Hour after hour, since I wrote the headlines of this chapter, my mind has been held in the same reverential awe. I have written and preached much on the Holy Spirit, for the knowledge of Him has been the most vital fact of my experience. I owe everything to the gift of Pentecost. It came to me when I was not seeking it. It came along the line of duty, in the crisis of obedience. There came into my soul a deep peace, a thrilling joy, and a new sense of power. There was a new sense of spring and vitality, a new power of endurance, and a strong man's exhilaration in big things. The wind and the fire and the tongues excited most comment, but they vanished, and it was the realities that remained that were the most wonderful. Pentecost gave me the key to the Scriptures. It has kept me in all the slippery places of all sorts of criticism. The inexplicable becomes plain when we recognise the Presence and Law of the Spirit. Learning without the Holy Ghost blinds men to the realities of Divine truth. The man who thinks he can know the Word of God by mere intellectual study is greatly deceived. The same Spirit gave me a new understanding and experience of prayer, and with these gifts there came a new enduement of wisdom and power. From the first day of my Pentecost I became a seeker and a winner of souls.

Chadwick goes on and shows that the baptism with the Spirit is a definite experience and shows that the New Testament is replete with Spirit baptism. The disciples were commanded to 'Tarry until they were endued with power from on high' (Luke 24:49). Of the believers at Samaria it was said that when Peter and John came down they prayed for them that they might receive the Holy Ghost (Acts 8:15). The question of Paul to the converts of Apollos implies that is is possible to be born again but not yet filled with the Spirit (Acts 19:1-6). The Spirit fills, vitalises, and energises in service with the power of God. Deliverance from sin, efficiency in service, and effectiveness in witnessing are given with the fullness of the Pentecostal blessing. Power to move the world for God and to win souls for Him is neither intellectual nor social, but is in the fullness of the Spirit of God in the soul. 'Ye shall receive power, after that the Holy Ghost is come upon you' (Acts 1:8).

The Pentecostal blessing makes the believer mighty in prayer. 'In that day ye shall ask in My Name.... and whatsoever ye shall ask the Father in My Name He give you' (John 15:16). Prayer is an impossible task without the Holy Spirit. There are two kinds of praying. Before Pentecost we pray in the Spirit; after Pentecost the Spirit prays through us. None but the Spirit-filled know that kind of praying. It is the kind that wrought miracles in the Acts of the Apostles, and to this day prevails. It pleads the Name, enthrones the Name, and claims the Name. It prays His will, presents His promise, and decrees in His power. The Spirit instructs and inspires prayer, gives intelligence and intensity to intercession and brings reality and joy to communion with God. The Spirit-filled love to pray, and prayer that is in the Spirit must prevail. Chadwick is progressive to the inheritance of the Spirit-filled life and shows Rom. 8 is the fullest exposition of the life which comes through 'the Spirit of Life in Christ Jesus' (Rom. 8:2). It is the charter of the believer's inheritance in the Spirit.

(1) Pentecost brings Deliverance. The law of the Spirit of Life in Christ Jesus makes men and women free. He breaks the power of cancelled sin. It is the Gospel of Liberty to all imprisoned life. There is no slave the Gospel cannot save. The greatest deliverance of all is from the moral impotence of the dual personality of chapter seven. 'There is therefore now no condemnation to them that are in Christ Jesus' (Rom. 8:1).

(2) Pentecost brings Abounding Vitality. Our Lord came that we might have abundant and abounding life, and it is found in the Gift of the Spirit of Life. The Gift of God is Living Water, springing up into everlasting life. The Spirit of Life dwells in men and women, permeates their being, sanctifies their nature, quickens their powers, vitalises their mortal bodies, and radiates their life. They live – really live! Pentecost wakens people up. It vitalises latent powers, and makes the utmost of every faculty and gift. Those who would have Life – abounding Life, victorious Life, satisfying Life, glorious Life – must get to Pentecost. It cures all ills, ends all weariness and conquers death all the time.

(3) Pentecost brings Understanding. Where did Peter get the sermon he preached on the Day of Pentecost? Who taught him? How did he know the hidden meaning of Prophecy? He knew by the Spirit of Wisdom and Revelation. The Spirit of Truth guides into all truth. We know, and do not despair. We know God. We know that at the last we shall be saved, and shall stand approved in Christ at the Throne of God. None shall lay anything to the charge of God's elect. Nothing shall separate us from the love of God. 'In that Day ye shall know.' The Spirit is familiar with the deep things of God, and He takes of the things of Christ and reveals them unto those who receive Him. He makes men wise with the wisdom that is from above.

(4) Pentecost brings a New Fellowship in Prayer. 'And in like manner the Spirit also helpeth our infirmity: for we know not how to pray as we ought; but the Spirit Himself maketh intercession for us with groanings that cannot be uttered; and He that searcheth the hearts knoweth what is the mind of the Spirit, because He maketh intercession for the saints according to the will of God' (Rom. 8:26).

(5) Pentecost brings Power. That was the specific promise of Christ. 'Ye shall receive Power after that the Holy Ghost is come upon you, and ye shall be witnesses unto Me' (Acts 1:8). 'And they overcame him (Satan) because of the blood of the Lamb, and because of the word of their testimony, and they loved not their lives unto death' (Rev. 12:11). The Spirit of Power is given for witnessing. The testimony of Pentecost was mighty. It is always mighty in the demonstration of the Spirit.

(6) Pentecost brings the Fire of God. Fire is the chosen symbol of Heaven for moral passion. It is emotion aflame. The Holy Spirit baptises in fire. Spirit-filled souls are ablaze for God. They love with a love that glows. They believe with a faith that kindles. They serve with a devotion that consumes. They hate sin with a fierceness that burns. They rejoice with a joy that radiates. Love is perfected in the Fire of God. Nothing can separate us from the love of God.

(7) Pentecost brings Passion for the Souls of Men. The eighth chapter overflows into the ninth. The experience consummates in anguish and tears for the lost. There is no sterner test of Grace than the attitude to the lost. Pentecost leads back to Gethsemane, for it baptises into Christ's Baptism of Redeeming Passion. Spirit-filled hearts are always tender, and they see men and women through the tears of a holy compassion.

In chapter 8 of his book, *The Way to Pentecost*, Chadwick deals with 'The Communion Of The Holy Ghost.' Communion means partnership and the word is used in the New Testament by those who are in fellowship with God. In Luke 5:10 it is said that James and John, sons of Zebedee, were partners with Simon. Paul says of Titus that he was his partner and fellow-labourer (2 Cor. 8:23). Of Philemon and Onesimus it is used in the still more intimate sense of comradeship. We are called of God 'into the fellowship of His Son Jesus Christ our Lord' (1 Cor. 1:9). Through Him we 'become partakers of the divine Nature' (2 Pet. 1:4). The Christian Benediction ascribes Love to the Father, Grace to the Son, and Communion to the Holy Ghost. The Spirit is the executive agent of the Father and the Son. He brings us into the fellowship of the Father and the Son by entering into communion with us. The negotiations are from Him, the consent is with us. There are no reserves with Him. He is straightened in us, for all His negotiations wait for our consent.

> The Spirit of God is not the monopoly of any particular class. There is nothing done by the minister that may not be done by anyone to whom the Holy Spirit is given. He is my Helper, my Witness, my Teacher, my Guide, my Strength.... The communion of the Spirit is with us. His resources are inexhaustible, and His power invincible, but! but! But! There are reserves, conditions, interests; barriers that hinder, grieve, and quench the Spirit. He is held up by the barriers of unbelief, and prayerless living, worldly ambition, stupid vanity, and inflated pride. He longs for our fellowship. For the sake of Christ and the Kingdom of Grace, He longs to be admitted to confidence and co-operation. He wants a central place in our hearts, and to be admitted to the life of the soul. He comes to co-operate, and co-operation waits for confidence and consent. All the conditions of power are met in the supply of the Spirit. Personality is quickened and sanctified. Sympathy is deepened

> and enlightened, and in sympathy are the discernment that understands and the appeal that woos and wins. Weakness becomes strength when the Spirit of Might comes upon us. Ordinary men and women become wonderful when clothed with Spirit of Power.

Weakness is a reproach when such might is at our service. Defeat is dishonour when the partnership of God is rejected. With the communion of the Holy Ghost at our command, what manner of men we ought to be. With such a partnership what mighty works we ought to do. There are no limits to His power. There is no respect of persons with Him. Sign the deed today, and there will come the joy and power of the Holy Spirit of God who is the Spirit of Christ. The grace of our Lord Jesus Christ, and the love of God, and the communion of the Holy Spirit be with you all.

Samuel Chadwick then turns to authority in the New Testament and Chapter 10 of his book is 'The Spirit of Power.' There is probably no instinct of the heart so strong as the craving for the sovereignty of power. Might is the attribute of God most coveted of men. 'Ye shall be as God,' was the appeal that prevailed, and its success was in the fact that it appealed to the craving for sovereignty. Man was made for thrones and dominion. He snatched at it and fell. Even then the instinct for power remained. It is the dominant passion of the human race and the key to its history. The determination to possess it is responsible for more than half the bloodshed of the world, and its urge has been the dynamic of civilisation in all ages. The kingdoms of this world are built on the love of power. Satan's way to thrones and dominion is by the assertion for self-realisation; God's way is by the surrender of self on the altar of sacrifice. Calvary is God's way. In the Kingdom of Heaven the Bleeding Lamb is in the midst of the Throne. The way to sovereignty is by the way of the Cross. The badge of authority is service, the mark of distinction is humility, and the right to rule is the power to obey.

> The gift of power is the gift of personality. It turns ordinary persons into extraordinary personalities. That is the miracle of Pentecost.... Our Lord to His disciples, 'Behold, I send forth the promise of My Father upon you; tarry ye in the city, until ye be clothed with power from on high'

> (Luke 24:49).... Every kind of power comes in the Spirit; intellectual power, moral power, spiritual power, and physical power. That is the Personality of Pentecost. He is the Spirit of Truth, the Spirit of Holiness, and the Spirit of Power. He quickens the mind, purifies the heart, and strengthens the whole man. Power! Power belongeth to God, and in the gift of the Spirit. He makes all grace abound to us, that we, having sufficiency in all things, may abound unto every good work. Power! All things are possible to those who have power. Power! The supreme need of man and the crowning gift of God is Power; power to conquer, power to attain, power to achieve. The Spirit of God is the Spirit of Power.[53]

The atmosphere of the Apostolic Church is charged with Divine Power. Their word was with power and conviction accompanied their speech. Signs and wonders confirmed their testimony. They uncovered the hearts of evil doers and Heaven put its seal upon their judgements. Rulers trembled in their presence. The dead heard their voice and disease fled at their touch. They were sure of the mind of God, for they were taught of the Spirit. They asked and received for they prayed in the Spirit. They wrought mighty works for they were strengthened in the might of the Spirit. The normal life of the Church was filled, inspired and empowered in the fullness of the Spirit of the living God. All the causes of our failure go back to this one common source: do we believe in the Holy Ghost, the Spirit of Truth, the Lord and Giver of Life? Without His guidance wisdom gropes in darkness and without His strength there is no might. The salvation of the world is 'not by might, nor by power, but by My Spirit, saith the Lord of Hosts' (Zech. 4:6). There is no straitening in Him. The reason of our failure is not in Him. He is straitened in us.

In chapter eleven of his book, 'The Spirit of Life,' Chadwick speaks about life is the gift of God in Christ Jesus and the Divine Spirit is the Spirit of Life. Life has its seat in man's spiritual nature, in his self-conscious reason, his moral sense, and his capacity for the knowledge of and fellowship with God. The Spirit of God quickens into life the Spirit of man. The body of man in the temple of the Holy Ghost, but

---

[53] Samuel Chadwick, *The Way to Pentecost*, p.59.

He does not dwell in the flesh. Spirit dwell in spirit. The Spirit of God dwells in the spirit of man, and from that centre of life and power He quickens, directs, controls and sanctifies the whole man. He indwells sanctified men and women. He becomes the spirit of their spirit, the mind of their mind, the heart of their heart, the strength of their strength, and the life of their life.

> All Christ-likeness of life and character is by the transforming power of Life through the Spirit of the Living God, the Lord and Giver of Life. That is why the work of God in the Church depends upon the Life of the Church. The City of the Living God comes through the Spirit of the Living God. That is why an ecclesiastical dignitary may know less about conversion than a Hallelujah lass of the Salvation Army. It is not by might of carnal strength, nor in the power of organised authority, but by the Spirit of the Lord.... The believer is born of the Spirit, he believes in the Spirit, prays in the Spirit, and walks in the Spirit. Delivered from the flesh, he lives in the Spirit. It is a life in which there is no condemnation. Guilt is purged, sin is cleansed away, carnality is destroyed. There is not only an imputed righteousness by grace, but a realised righteousness through faith.... The Spirit of Christ brings the mind of Christ, and baptises us into the fellowship of His redeeming love. This is the abundant life Christ came to bring – the life filled with His Spirit.[54]

In chapter thirteen of his book, *The Way to Pentecost*, Samuel Chadwick says some important things about 'The Spirit of Holiness.' It's eighty-five years since this book was published and he gives counsel over what has divided some people on this topic. The Resurrection of our Lord is attributed to the Holy Spirit; and even if it be the quality of our Lord's own Spirit that made it impossible that He should be holden of death, the human spirit was equipped, sanctified, and kept by the Divine Spirit. The phrase, however, reaches further than the Resurrection, and implies that, by the Spirit of Holiness, men are sanctified in truth. His work is to glorify Christ and sanctify the saints, making holy the Body of Christ which is His Church.

> It is unfortunate that the term holiness has ceased to attract even good people. There are some who regard it with suspicion, and some who

---

[54] Samuel Chadwick, *The Way to Pentecost*, p.71.

dismiss it with scorn. It is not uncommon for it to be made the butt of cheap wit and the subject of some doubtful stories. This is all the more surprising because of the emphasis with which the New Testament insists upon its necessity, urges its experience, and enforces its obligation. There is little teaching and testimony on the subject, and, therefore, there is dense ignorance and much misunderstanding. The subject is generally dismissed without inquiry; but even among those who take the trouble to think there is much misapprehension, and the reason is that due attention is not given to the place and work of the Holy Spirit in the sanctification of the Believer. He is the Sanctifier.

The meaning of holiness must be interpreted according to the Scriptures. It has a Biblical content and value. Its root meaning is separation, and it was used of things dedicated to religious uses. He chose them to be unto Him a holy people. They were to be unto Him 'a peculiar people,' in whom all men should see a holy and sanctified people. Holiness is an experience as well as an attitude, a life as well as a separation. The supreme revelation and standard are in Jesus Christ. He revealed the Holy Father and made manifest the Holy Spirit, thereby making known in both God and man the Spirit of Holiness. Believers are called unto holiness. 'This is the will of God, even your sanctification' (1 Thess. 4:3). 'God chose you from the beginning in sanctification of the Spirit' (2 Thess. 2:13). Without holiness grace fails in its purpose, and without it no man can see the Lord. Holiness is an attitude of dedication and an experience of grace in which the heart is cleansed from sin and made perfect in love.[55]

There is a strange mistake abroad that holiness is something quite optional. It is regarded as desirable and in special circumstances, but its claims are by no means universal. Holiness is regarded as an emotional luxury, if not as a spiritual fad. Many take it for granted that if it is necessary it will come to them in due course without any concern of theirs. Such slackness accounts for much of the backsliding among believers. The Christian calling is one that demands all diligence and earnest heed.

---

55 Samuel Chadwick, *The Way to Pentecost*, pp.73, 74.

Another mistake made by many earnest Christians about holiness is that it comes by gradual growth in grace and a steady progress of spiritual discipline. They are always growing toward it, but they never get into it, always struggling and striving to attain, but never entering into possession. The positive expectation is always seen to be afar off, and they die without having possessed. The hopeful future never becomes the positive now.... Growth is the result of health; holiness is the gift of abundant life. Growth is the result of health; holiness is health. Holiness implies a crisis, a new experience, a transformed life. It is not an achievement or attainment, but a gift of grace in the Holy Ghost. It comes not by works, but of faith.

The Scriptural method of sanctification is through the personal work of the Spirit of God. The law of the Spirit of life makes us free from the law of sin and death. It is God's work wrought in the heart by the Holy Spirit who makes Christ our sanctification. The way of life must be sought in the Holy Word and by the Holy Spirit and the twofold guide will not fail those who seek with all their heart. Holiness is in the spirit and of the Divine Spirit. It is not in prohibitions and self-denial. It is a spirit, a life, a principle, a dynamic. The Spirit of God indwells the spirit of man. He clothes Himself with man, and man is clothed in the presence and power of the Spirit. The Body is the Temple of the Spirit. Christ lives in men and women through the Spirit. He is no longer a model but a living Presence. Christian faith does not copy Him; it lives Him. Christ is not imitated but reproduced. Life is sanctified because He possesses it, lives it, transforms it. The Spirit of God does not work upon us; He lives in us. Holiness makes life fruitful because it abides in the Living Word and gives free scope to the Spirit of Life. The Spirit of Holiness makes the heart clean, the mind true, the faculties fit, and the life fruitful by making His holiness ours.

Samuel Chadwick, in his book, *The Way to Pentecost*, calls chapter fifteen, 'The Spirit Of Fire,' and opens with a statement.

> Our God is a consuming fire (Heb. 12:29). The elect symbol of his presence is the fire unkindled of earth, and the chosen sign of His approval is the sacred flame. Covenant and sacrifice, sanctuary and dispensation were sanctification and approved by the descent of fire.

'The God that answereth by fire, He is God' (1 Kings 18:24). This is the final universal test of deity. Jesus Christ came to bring fire upon the earth. The symbol of Christianity is not a Cross but a Tongue of Fire. So universal is this recognised that men substitute fire for the fire of God. A fireless altar is the sign of desertion and death. It means that the Temple has lost its God, and worship has died out of the land. Earth-fires can soon be set ablaze. It is much easier to excite the passion than to kindle souls. The penalty of strange fire in the sanctuary is death. Earth-kindled fires burn fiercely but they burn out. Artificial excitement destroys spiritual sensibility. Satiated desire fails. When religion turns to humanity for its inspiration and to the world for its power, God is dethroned and the sanctuary becomes a secularised fellowship.[56]

Strange fire may be offered in sincerity and in good faith. Stage fire is a trick. In the absence of the supernatural earnest souls may turn to the best substitutes they can find and believe they are doing God's service. When the fires of spiritual devotion go out, ritualism finds its opportunity. Churches destitute of divine fire may devote themselves fervently to good works, but stage fire is a mockery and a pretence. Stage-lights have found their way into the Church. The red glare dazzles but it does not burn. Fireworks are brilliant but they end with the hour. No ideals are kindled, no ministry impelled, no sacrifice inspired. The pretence of spirituality is the worst profanity. Strange fire is less offensive than stage fire. A religion of mere emotion and sensationalism is the most terrible of all curses that can come upon any people. The absence of reality is sad enough, but the aggravation of pretence is a deadly sin.

What is the fire of the Holy Ghost? Everywhere earnest believers are lamenting its absence and praying for a Pentecostal Fire. What is this Fire? The Scriptures evidently regard it as the supreme need of the Church and the final gift of God. The prophets associated it with the Messiah and promised it as the unique triumph of His coming. It marked the difference between the Old Testament and the New. John's ministry shook the nation, but was only preparatory. 'I indeed baptise with water.... He shall baptise you with the Holy Ghost and with Fire' (Matt. 3:11). Our Lord spoke of the coming with Fire as the one purpose of His mission, and the fruit of His sufferings and death. 'I come to cast Fire on

[56] Samuel Chadwick, *The Way to Pentecost*, pp.81, 82.

> the earth' (Luke 12:49). The supreme need of the Church is Fire. The one persistent prayer of them that sigh and cry is for the fiery baptism of Pentecost. What do we mean by Fire? When Jesus promised the gift of Fire, what did He mean them to expect? For what does this elect symbol stand? Our God is a consuming Fire; the gift of the Holy Spirit is a baptism of Fire; Christianity is a religion of Fire; we are saved by Fire.... Men's souls were charged, saturated, enveloped, in the Spirit of God.... It kindles a fervent devotion to God, a passion for righteousness, and a consuming desire to seek and save the lost. Religion at flame-heat illumines the mind, energises every faculty, and impassions every element of compassion.[57]

Chadwick goes on and spells out the offence of fire in religion. It is by a holy passion kindled in the soul we live the life of God. Truth without enthusiasm, morality without emotion, ritual without soul, are the things Christ unsparingly condemned. Destitute of fire they are nothing more than a godless philosophy, an ethical system, and a superstition. Moral and spiritual passion are of the essence of the religion of Christ. The pure flame of a holy enthusiasm is a safer guide than the dry light of cold reason. The soul's safety is in its heat. Fire is the best defence against corruption. Our religion is only secure when it is guarded by a wall of Fire round about. It is Fire that prevails. For fifty days the facts of the Gospel were complete but no conversions were recorded. Pentecost registered three thousand souls. It is the cause that sets men and women ablaze that wins converts. John Wesley, George Whitefield and General Booth wrought wonders by the Fire kindled of the Holy Ghost. Men ablaze are invincible and hell trembles when men kindle. Sin, worldliness, unbelief, hell, are proof against everything but Fire. The Church is powerless without the Fire of the Holy Ghost. The one vital need is Fire. One thing we know: it comes only with the presence of the Spirit of God, Himself the Spirit of Fire. God alone can send the Fire. It is His Pentecostal gift.

In his book, *The Way to Pentecost,* Samuel Chadwick deals with 'The Challenge Of Pentecost,' and all that it brings to the soul. Pentecost challenges the very citadel of our faith. The gift of the Spirit is the

---

57 Samuel Chadwick, *The Way to Pentecost*, pp.83, 84.

distinguishing feature of the Christian religion. In His indwelling Presence is the secret of all Christian experience, and in the abiding energy of His power is the dynamic of all Christian service. The blessing of Pentecost is the blessing of fullness. Fire, power, courage, and joy had their source in the fullness of the indwelling Spirit. The blessing affects the whole being. The seat of the Indwelling Presence is the innermost recesses of the spiritual being, but it permeates, energises, and controls every faculty of our nature. It is another Incarnation of which the Body is the consecrated believer. The Holy Ghost clothed Himself with the waiting disciples in the Upper Room, and He still clothes Himself with consecrated believers. Without confusion, without loss of personal consciousness, without change of inherent qualities, there are mutual appropriation and oneness of operation.

Something had happened between the Judgement Hall and the streets of the city. Resurrection found them all shivering behind closed doors for fear of the Jews, but at Pentecost they were openly preaching Jesus and charging the rulers with His death. Pentecost transformed them and it was the fullness that made the difference between timidity and joyous daring, shivering weakness and the exultant power. How does the challenge find us? Do we measure up to the standard of the fullness of Pentecost? Is not the explanation of our confusion in the lack of it? What about our assurance of heavenly things? There is an end of uncertainty when the fullness of Pentecost is known.

Chadwick then challenges us about the joy and blessing of being afraid that the world would hold us back from claiming the blessing.

> The Spirit of Truth is the Spirit of Holiness. The Day of Pentecost changed carnal thought into spiritual vision, pride into humility, selfishness into love, and cowardice into courage. It changed hearts and transformed lives. Victory comes by fullness. Have we the joy of conquest over sin? Is the character of the average Christian anywhere near the standard of a Spirit-filled soul? What about the love of the world? What has come of the doctrine of separation? If believers were filled with the Spirit, would they haunt the world's gaudy fountains?

> There is no doubt that the one thing needful for the Church is the blessing of Pentecostal fullness. The flood would take away all the rubbish, fill the dykes, and fertilise the desert.... The blessing is for all, and for all now. The conditions are simple, unalterable and universal. God waits to fill ordinary people with extraordinary power. Ask Peter and James and John. They had left all for Christ's sake, but were still without Pentecost. They were workers: stewards, preachers, evangelists, workers of miracles, without Pentecost. Then they heard the Promise of the Spirit, and set themselves to claim, wait and pray, and according to the Word the Spirit came, and they were all filled with the Holy Ghost.[58]

Samuel Chadwick rightly entitles his final chapter, *The Way Into The Blessing*, and starts by pointing out that many Christians have not the blessings because they ask amiss. They yearn for a fullness of life in Christ that never comes. They pray and nothing happens. They seek and somehow always miss the way. It must be there for others have it; and it must be for them, for with God there is no respect of persons. So periodically there comes a sense of hunger and a deep want of soul, and here the quest begins, and again the way is missed.

> Almost every day I get letters from people asking the way into the blessing. They probably represent a great host, and I am going to try to help them, even though I must begin with the confession that my own plea for help brought me nothing but confusion. Sometimes I was led to leave all books and interpreters, and give myself up to a search of the Scriptures, believing that God would make the truth known to me.... The way I came is the way I know. That is why I send every seeker to the Word of God, in dependence upon the Holy Spirit of Truth. The Blessing is known by many names, and is often confused with other experiences of Grace. It is known as the Pentecostal Gift of the Spirit, as Entire Sanctification, Christian Perfection, and Perfect Love.... There is Perfection that is definite, decisive, and determinate; the carnal mind, the body of sin, is done away. That is the Bible word for what happens – sin is done away. The fullness of the indwelling Spirit sanctifies and quickens every natural faculty, and bestows gifts that are peculiarly His own. Love is made perfect, and the sanctified will is energised by Divine Power.[59]

---

[58] Samuel Chadwick, *The Way to Pentecost*, pp.103, 104.

[59] Samuel Chadwick, *The Way to Pentecost*, p.106.

Salvation from first to last is of Grace through Faith. We are Justified by Faith, Sanctified by Faith, Spirit-filled by Faith. This second experience of Grace is the Gift of God through Faith unto Faith. Consider the commands of God that we must be holy. Search out the promises of God that we shall be holy. Pray through the prayers in the New Testament which set forth the Spirit-inspired pleadings for Holiness. The children of light walk in the light, and in obedience to the light there is conscious fellowship with the God of Life, Light and Love, 'and the Blood of Jesus Christ His Son cleanseth us from all sin' (1 John: 1:7). It is no business of ours to go scenting idols for the burning, but the Spirit searches every honest seeker and convicts, condemns, and commands; and there is generally a bonfire when the Fire of God falls. Chadwick points out that there are steps of faith that we must observe if we would be candidates for the blessing. Two things are plain. (1) Pentecost is a definite work of the Spirit in believers. (2) It is by grace through faith.

The first step is to repent. There is a repentance of believers as well as of sinners. Things not surrendered, indulgences retained against light, possessions held for selfish ends – these must all be surrendered to the supreme authority of Christ. For until He is exalted, crowned, glorified, there can be no Pentecost.

The second step is to ask. 'If ye then, being evil, know how to give good gifts unto your children, how much more shall your Heavenly Father give the Holy Spirit to them that ask Him' (Luke 11:13). The pleasures may be lawful and laudable enough, but God will not give the glory of His Son to another, and the mission of the Spirit is to glorify the Son. If the power is sought for success in Christian service merely, it will not be given. Christ must be supreme in affection and aim.

The third step is to receive. When the consecration is complete, the act of faith is quite simple. 'Receive ye the Holy Ghost' (John 20:22), is the all-inclusive command. It is the word used in the Upper Room, when our Lord gave them the bread that symbolised His Body – 'Take.' Faith claims and takes.

> The fourth step is the continuous life of obedience. Jesus Christ identifies faith and obedience, and in the Acts of the Apostles obedience is made of receiving and retaining the Spirit. 'And we are witnesses of these things, and so is the Holy Ghost, whom God has given to them that obey Him' (Acts 5:32). The blessing of Pentecost may be lost, and it is always lost, when obedience fails. The Spirit-filled must be Spirit-ruled. Those who are greatly used of God have no monopoly of the Holy Ghost; they are mighty through God because the Spirit has a monopoly of them. Again I say this extraordinary gift is for ordinary people. All may be filled as full and as truly as the hundred and twenty on the day of Pentecost. The conditions are the same for all: Repent, Ask, Receive, Obey.[60]

The second book by Samuel Chadwick appeared in 1960 and it bore the title, *Through the Year with Samuel Chadwick*, compiled by D. W. Lambert. It marked the hundred years since Chadwick was born and its compilation was undertaken by D.W. Lambert. He and Chadwick had worked together at Cliff College and for seven years he went with Chadwick into the class-room and Chadwick called him his 'Black-rod.' Lambert was responsible for, *25 Sunday Mornings with Samuel Chadwick* (1951); *Twenty-Five Sunday Evenings with Samuel Chadwick* (1954); *The Testament of Samuel Chadwick: 1860-1932* (1957). Lambert has arranged these readings into fifty-six and called them, 'Devotional Readings for Every Sunday of the Year.' Paying tribute to Chadwick as a man of deep devotions and a leading figure in the Christian world, he wrote a Foreword and pays tribute to one who was a soul-winner both in Church work and then as a Cliff College Principal from 1912 to 1932.

> This book is a Centenary tribute. Samuel Chadwick was born in Burnley on 16th September, 1860, and became a leading figure in the Christian world. He was a great preacher, a mighty evangelist, a prophetic leader of the Free Churches, and especially of his beloved Methodism. It is as a devotional writer that we would especially remember him. His front-page articles in the *Joyful News* are full of deep devotional teaching.

---

60 Samuel Chadwick, *The Way to Pentecost,* p.110.

The Church calendar has been used and this has served as a guide in the choice of subjects. We trust that these readings will give some clue to the wealth of spiritual teaching that flowed from the pen of Samuel Chadwick. May they bring blessings and inspiration to many.[61]

Second Sunday in Advent

The Birth That Killed Death
Hebrews 2:12-18

He became Man that He might die for men, and 'that through death He might destroy him that had the power of death, that is, the devil; and deliver them who through fear of death were all their lifetime subject to bondage.' Angels cannot die for men, so He took not the nature of angels. He came to die. Others came into the world to live, but 'He Himself took part in flesh and blood, that through death' might accomplish man's deliverance from the bondage of death. The Son of God became the Son of Man, that He might face man's foe and bring man back to God. The fact of sin is in all the fibre of Revealed Truth. If the Bible is wrong about sin, it is right about nothing. The issue of sin is death. The soul that sins dies. Death originated in sin: that is, death as the human race knows it. Satan reigned over the kingdom of death. He is said to have had 'The power of death.' Not that death was under his control, but he is lord in the realm of sin and the empire of death. Christ came to destroy him and deliver his victims from the bondage of fear. To destroy means to 'make of none effect,' and our Lord by His death has robbed Satan of his power and death of its terror. The sting of death is sin, and Jesus by His atoning death has taken away sin and its guilt.

The incarnate-God could not be holden of death, and He saves by the power of an endless life. The gift of God is Eternal life. Those who are in Christ are delivered from the fear of death because they do not die. It is true that it is still appointed unto all men once to die, and it is also true that those who 'eat and drink of the Flesh and Blood of the Son of God' cannot see death, for they have eternal life. There is in all living beings an instinctive fear of dying, and to the saint there is a death that causes sorrow but no fear. When Christ spake of His own death, He said He was going Home to His Father. The Birth of the Manger has transformed the Grave into the Gateway of life. There were angels at the Manger,

61 D.W. Lambert, 'Foreword', *Through the Year with Samuel Chadwick*, p.11.

and there were angels in the Tomb. As both they were the Messengers of Life. The message of Christmas is the message of Life, Divine Life, Victorious Life, Abundant Life, Eternal Life. Christ's birthday is the birthday of the world.

Fourth Sunday in Advent

Heaven's Bethlehem Song
Revelation 7:9-17; 12:1-5

The angels sang over the plains of Bethlehem the message of the Incarnation. It was a glorious song of Glory and Peace and Goodwill. The song set the sermon to music. To John on Patmos it was given to hear the song they sang in Heaven. And this is the song: 'Now is come the salvation, and the power, and the Kingdom of our God, and the authority of His Christ: For the accuser of our brethren is cast down, which accuseth them before our God day and night. And they overcame him because of the Blood of the Lamb, and because of the word of their testimony; and they loved not their life even unto death. Therefore rejoice, O heavens, and ye that dwell therein.' They sing of Salvation that came not to the Jews, but to all people, all ages and all worlds.

The heavenly Bethlehem makes bigger demands on our faith than the earthly story. It is no longer the wonderful story of the birth of the Christ-Child in fulfilment of prophecy amid circumstances so pathetic in their poverty and signs so wonderfully in their majesty. The Manger is a Stable, the Song of the Angels, the homage of the Wise Men, and the enmity of Herod will carry our minds and hearts to Bethlehem with every return of the Christmas festival. The wranglings of controversy will never silence the song of the Angels or destroy the wonder of worship. We shall still go to Bethlehem and there is every reason that we should, but Bethlehem is the starting-point for Patmos and the of the Nativity of Heaven. In this also we know not Christ after the flesh. The faith of Bethlehem is perfected and verified in the vision of things within the veil. Heaven sets the scene in the eternal. The Christ that was born of a Woman was before Abraham, before Creation, eternal with God. He was, and is, and is to come. All centres in Him. All power dwells in Him. All grace is from Him. In Him is the Life that gives that gives Life and is Light. Salvation, Eternal, Universal Salvation is secured in Him. He must reign. The Kingdom is given to the Son. Where they see the end from the beginning they sing the Salvation that is *now*! When they see we believe, and join their song.

Sexagesima Sunday
To What Extent Is Jesus Able To Save?

Hebrews 7:22-28

The writer to the Hebrews says He is able to save to the uttermost (7:25). The uttermost what? The uttermost is the utmost limit of a thing. Salvation to the uttermost saves to the utmost limit where sin lurks or its evil remains. St. Paul speaks of the breadth, and length, and depth, and height, of the love of God which passeth knowledge. The same measurement applies to the uttermost salvation in which we know the immeasurable love. He is able to save to the uttermost depth. That does not mean He is able to save the sinner that has sunk the lowest; though that is true. It means the uttermost depths of our nature where lie the hidden and unknown things of our being. Who can understand his errors, or sound the possibilities for good or ill that lie in the depth of his soul? The heart is deceitful above all things. The Psalmist prays for cleansing from hidden faults; not the secret things he had hidden but the hidden things of which he was not aware. He is able to save to the uttermost depths, and to cleanse our blood.

What about the uttermost heights? Who can measure them? Who dare limit them? He is able to do exceedingly above all we can ask or think. What is the uttermost length? From the beginning, all the way, to the uttermost, and right on over the River, and all through eternity in the Celestial City. He is able, whatever the perils and hardships of the way to save to the uttermost, and he that endureth to the end shall be saved. 'Wherefore He is able to save them to the uttermost that come unto God by Him, seeing He ever liveth to make intercession for them.'

Fourth Sunday in Lent

The Bleeding Lamb

John 2:29-34

The Cross is the manifestation in time of an eternal and universal fact of creation. There is no Cross in heaven, but there is Lamb, and we have an Altar. God sprinkled the doorpost of creation, before they were sprinkled in Egypt. The Bleeding Lamb is in the midst of the Eternal Throne, in the midst of Creation, and in the midst of the Angels, as well as in the midst of the Redeemer. The Lamb is on the Throne, which means that Sacrifice is the Supreme and eternal law of life. The Lamb is on the Throne, which means that sacrifice is the foundation of the world as well as from it. He was a Lamb without blemish and without spot, who verily was fore-ordained before the foundation of the world. There was a fore-ordination before Creation. When there was none but God, three Persons, One God, there was the Lamb of God. That must mean that sacrifice is the essential principle of the Divine Nature. The Lamb was in the Godhead from before the beginning. The Lamb is eternal. God redeemed the Church with His own blood. The blood of the Lamb is the Blood of God. The Blood is the life. He gave himself. The Lamb is of God as the Logos was of God. In the beginning was the Lamb, and Lamb was with God, and the Lamb was God; and the Lamb of God taketh away the sin of the world. He is the Sin-Bearer and the Saviour of the world.

Not all the blood of beasts
On Jewish altars slain
Could give the guilty conscience peace
Or wash away our stain.

But Christ, the heavenly Lamb
Takes all our sins away
A sacrifice of nobler name
And richer blood than they.

Isaac Watts

Ascension Day
On The Mount of Ascension

Mark 16:14-20

Jesus met His disciples on Ascension Day by appointment. They had returned to Galilee as He had told them. They had kept more or less together, and from time to time Jesus had revealed Himself unexpectedly and in different forms. There had been no appointed place at which they could be sure He would come to them, but on this day there was a place fixed and a promised day given. They gathered together on the hill expecting and wondering. The Eleven were there and no more. He came to them. They knew Him, though in some hearts there were misgivings, but as He came to them they all fell at His feet in adoring worship. No man spoke. Their disquieting questions found no speech. He spake. The urge of the Spirit was upon Him, and he spake as He spake as He had never spoken before. There was much to be said and the Father's chariot waited. Write out His words from each Gospel and the first chapter of the Acts of the Apostles, and note the tone and scope of His authority and His promises. Compare the Mount of Ascension with the Mount of Temptation. See how His mission goes beyond the boundaries of Israel to the whole world and all creation. Note how, instead of sending them forth by twos into hamlets and villages, they were to become His evangelists, ambassadors, and teachers to every nation under heaven. Hear the ring of victory in His promises; His presence, His Protection, His Power. He added another symbol, by which the citizens of His Kingdom should be in a living fellowship in all ages throughout the world. A little drop of water! Baptism by water in the glorious Name of the Blessed Trinity was to be the entrance-symbol of all His people. A little water, a little bread, a little wine, nothing more! The same word included all: 'Lo, I am with you all the days, even unto the end of the world. Amen,' (Matt. 28:20).

Whit Sunday

The Baptism of Fire
Acts 2:1-4

Such a baptism of fire refines and sanctifies all our life, throwing its halo over business, devotion, and recreation alike, so that every act and every thought reflects the image of our Lord. Is it not plain that this is our great need? There is plenty of liberality and self-denying effort, there is great interest in all kinds of religious subjects, there is genial tolerance and wide culture, there is a high standard of morality, but there is little love and little fire. All the evils we have to mourn among the churches spring from the absence of this Spirit of burning. Our decorous coldness is our curse, both in pulpit and in pew. When He maketh His ministers a flaming fire, and when upon all His members there abides this cloven tongue of flame, then will Zion arise in the fullness of her strength. Today we lack nothing but the fire.

At Pentecost the baptism came upon a prepared people. Peter was forgiven and restored, Thomas was no longer unbelieving, and all had waited in willing consecration at His feet for ten days. Are we ready? Some have not even received John's baptism as yet, and this must always come before the baptism of fire. Many have 'brought forth fruits for repentance', and are waiting for the baptism of the Spirit. Are we prepared to let the searching, sanctifying power to shine through us – lighting up every corner and crevice of our life, testing every motive, destroying every idol, startling with its fiery glare our secret sins, and wrapping its fiery tongue around every treasured wrong? Who among us can dwell with everlasting burnings? (Isaiah 33:14). No wonder Christ asked His disciples if they could be baptised with His baptism; but in a better spirit than theirs, we may confidently and sincerely say we can.

O that in me the sacred fire
Might now begin to glow.

Charles Wesley

Fifth Sunday after Trinity

What Happens To The Man In Christ?
2 Cor. 5:14-17

There is a new creation. God takes the natural man as He took the dust of the earth at the beginning, and breathes into him a new quality of life in the Person of His own Living Spirit. Man is re-born, and the birth is of God. He is not re-made out of the old material, but there is a new creation which makes a new man in Christ. The natural man is not destroyed, though there is an 'old man' that is crucified and done away. The new creation does not give a man a new body, but it makes the shrine, the home, and instrument of God. It does not give new brains, but it does give a new mind, which is the mind of Christ. It does not supersede personality, but it so sanctifies in that it creates a new man in Christ. The natural powers are so delivered from bondage and darkness, that they are endued with new capacity and understanding. There is a new creation with sin left out; a new nature in which no carnality remains; a new disposition in which the mind of God is supreme. It is difficult to explain just what happens, but it is something that none but God can do, and the result is a new man in Christ; a new creation which is the kingdom of God, a new sonship of God the Father, and a new kinship of the Holy Family of Christ.

The creative plan takes in every man. So the declaration is that 'if any man is in Christ, he is a new creature. 'Any man.' That means that any man may be in Christ. God despairs of none. The worst may be saved because salvation is a new creation, in which old things pass away and all things become new; and its sphere of operation is in Christ. In Him is a new disposition, a new mind, a new heart, a new life, and a new world.

Tenth Sunday after Trinity

Whatsoever Ye Shall Ask In My Name
John 17:21-26

The modern apologist for Prayer usually discards Prophets and Apostles and takes our Lord as the supreme Example and Teacher, but all Scripture is written for our learning. There is no controversy between them. Our Lord was much in Prayer, but we have little information about His Prayers. We know, however, that He asked definite petitions, and in Gethsemane He prayed the same prayer three times using the same words. He sweat at Prayer, even unto blood. Prayer is not the importunity of beggars, but the privilege of sons, and yet even the Son of God prayed with strong crying and tears. It is useless to ask why, because the reason is among the causes that reason does not know. It is not in the logic of law, but in the fellowship of Spirit. Even the Spirit of God groans in the fellowship of Prayer.

It is said the human mind cannot know how to pray or what to ask. That is true on the authority of Scripture, but it is only half the truth. The child of God knows both, for he is instructed by the Spirit of God who knows the deep things of God. Asking is not arbitrary. The man taught of the Spirit knows for what he can pray. He is instructed in the Will and Purpose of God, and when he is assured of these he prays with confidence. I believe there is nothing that concerns me about which I may not pray. The fact that God has the responsibility of creation, and the care of many creatures does not distress me, because to the Infinite, each must be as if there were no other. It is as if I were His one and only concern, and when I pray I expect to have His complete interest and attention, and I get it. Conflicting interests do not concern me; they are His concern, not mine. Jesus taught us to pray for our daily bread, and if we may pray for bread there is no material good for which we may not pray. So, whatever scientists and philosophers say, I shall go on praying to my Heavenly Father about every concern and need of my life, always asking in the Name of our Lord; and like Him I can say: 'I know that Thou hearest me always.'

Thirteenth Sunday after Trinity

Holiness A Way Of Life

Exodus 23:20-25; Isaiah 43:16-19

The point I want to emphasize is that Holiness is a way. Have you noticed how much the Bible has to say about ways? Those who have no way get nowhere. The people who lose their way perish. People get lost in deserts where there is nothing to see, and in forests where there is so much to see that one can see nothing. What a boon there is a way.

What is implied in a way? A way starts somewhere and goes somewhere. A way is made, certified, and kept. A way is guaranteed to all travellers. The King is responsible for it. The Way of Holiness is the Lord's way for His ransomed people. It starts at the Cross and ends in Glory. All roads in the Roman Empire led to the Golden Milestone in the City of Rome. So this road leads straight to Glory. The Roman roads had a character of their own. They were straight roads. They went straight over mountains, across rivers and deserts, swamps and forests, and they remain as symbols of the conquering power of the Caesars.

God's way bears the mark of His character. It is a Holy Way, the Lord's way for His people. It begins at a definite point, it is maintained according to His law, it proceeds to its appointed destination. Those who walk therein must respect its boundaries and obey its laws. Holiness is God's way of Life. The command is to follow after Holiness, 'without which no man can see the Lord.' The Holy way is for Holy people, and it leads to the glory of the Holy God. It is clean and it is plain; it is safe and it is companionable; it is in the Lord's keeping and it is sure.

Sixteenth Sunday after Trinity

Harps Of Prophetic Speech
Psalm 49:3, 4

The band of prophets came down from the hill of God 'with a psaltery, and a tabret, and a pipe, and a harp' (1 Sam. 10:3). Jeduthan prophesied with a harp (1 Chron. 25:3). The Psalmist said:
My mouth shall speak wisdom
And the meditation of my heart shall be of understanding.
I will incline mine ear to a parable
I will open my dark saying upon the harp (Psalm 49:3, 4).

There are musicians who can make anything talk. Music is speech. There is music that is vulgar, sensuous, immoral, secular; and there is music that is tender, noble, spiritual, sacred. The prophet speaks to the heart. He speaks of the deep things of God, of life, and of the world. He needs a harp. He speaks of mysteries profound and solemn, of issues momentous and eternal. He needs a harp. He speaks of love that passes knowledge, of peace that passes all understanding, of joy unspeakable, and full of glory. He needs a harp. No other instrument has range and depth enough for the testimony of the soul and the language of the heart. The trombone is too slow, the flute too thin, the drum too noisy, and the cymbal too shallow. Jazz is a blasphemy in the sanctuary of the soul. There must be adoring worship, reverence, thanksgiving, lowly penitence, radiant certainty, and tender entreaty in the prophecy of those who prophesy with the harp. Has modern prophesying lost its harp? One of the signs of desolation in the God-abandoned city was that there was no longer the voice of the harpers, minstrels, and trumpeters. What is wrong with modern preaching? Is it that the preachers have lost their harps?

Twentieth Sunday after Trinity

The Seed In The Life
1 Peter 1:22-25

Seed to fructify must be buried, must be quickened, must die, and must be nourished in newness of life. Otherwise it abideth alone. The Word of God is seed. It needs to be received by faith, implanted in the mind, and hidden in the heart. It is no use so long as it is merely in a book, even the Bible. The seed received with meekness springs up and brings forth after its kind. The seed of life is quickened by the Holy Spirit, who is the Lord and Giver of life. The Word is the medium and instrument of the Spirit. The Word is powerless without the Spirit, and the Spirit does nothing but by the Word. The two cannot be divided without disaster. Hence the Spirit is magnified to the neglect of the Word, there is a sure crop of fanaticism, wildfire, and moral disaster. On the other hand, if the Word of God is exalted to the neglect of the Holy Spirit, there is dead orthodoxy, formalism and persecution. The Spirit-filled life is by the Word of Truth, and the Spirit dwells where the Word abides. The Spirit convicts of sin by the Word of Truth. The New Birth is of the incorruptible seed which is by the Word of God. Faith cometh by hearing, and hearing by the Word of God. The Word of God is the warrant of faith, and the Word is a living, growing, fruit-bearing seed. Search the Scriptures and see the precious thing begotten of this divine seed. It cleanses and gives peace, rejoicing the heart and makes men wise, strengthens with might and guides the feet in the way of life. To neglect the Bible is to miss the richest and best, it is to miss the pearl of great price, and to miss the way of salvation. The Word of God is the Seed of God, and Christ is the Word that is God. He too must be planted. 'I in you, and ye in Me.'

All Saints' Day

Perection Through Fellowship
Hebrews 11:32-40; 12:1-2

We need them, and without us, they cannot be perfect. The law of mutuality runs through all the universe of God. It is true of earth, and it is true of heaven. The eternal finds expression through the Word made flesh, the Word finds interpretation and function in the Spirit, and the Spirit fulfils His Mission through the Church which is the Body of Christ. The members of the Body depend upon, and minister to, each other. No man lives to himself. Nothing can come to itself of itself. Whatever abides by itself alone must die. The Church is one in heaven and on earth. The saints in heaven serve, they grow in knowledge, and they develop by the training and exercise of their powers. There may be spheres of service of which we know nothing. Quite likely! We do know, however, that they and we are in the same fellowship of inheritance, privilege, and service. For 'we are come unto mount Zion, and unto the City of the Living God, the heavenly Jerusalem, and to innumerable hosts of angels, to the general assembly of the Church of the first-born who enrolled in Heaven, and to God the Judge the Judge of all, and to the spirits of just men made perfect, and to Jesus the Mediator of a new Covenant, and to the blood of sprinkling that speaketh better things than that of Abel' (Heb. 12:22-24). We have entered into the labours of those who rest from their labour. We owe it to them to reap what they have sown, and to complete the task for which they suffered and toiled. Apart from us their work cannot be made perfect.

There is perfection for them and for us. Heaven awaits the consummation of the Cross in the perfect glory of the Kingdom. The isolated shall be related, and the broken shall be complete. Labour shall find its reward and sorrow its meaning. Progress will be eternal and perfection in all things perfect. Eternity will perfect time, completeness will perfect discipline, glory will perfect grace, God will perfect all.

Twenty-fourth Sunday after Trinity

Narrowness The Law Of Life
Matthew 7:14-20

Our Lord's words have a wider application than religion. The Gateway of life is always narrow, and the way of life is always a narrow way. There is nothing so disastrous as dissipation. Whatever is lawless must perish. There are thrilling attractions in unfenced spaciousness and unfettered freedom, but space and wind make poor feeding. The Broad and the Narrow represent two ways of life, two principles of choice, two characters of people, and two ultimate destinies. There are but these two. They divide at the cross-roads, and at the cross-roads there is a Cross. The way of Christ is the way of the Strait Gate and the Narrow Way and the way of the Christian Church is the way of God. There is a social side to the ministry of Christ – of course there is, and there is a social ministry of the Church. No one denies that. There may even be a ministry of fun. In areas of social desolation, the Church feeds the hungry of body and of mind, heart and soul, but let it keep social service where Christ put it; and not mistake the bread that perisheth for the ministry of life. There is Good Tidings for the poor that is better than food and raiment, advancement and pleasure, security and betterment. God has set eternity in the heart of the poor, as well as of the rich. They misjudge men and women, old and young, who think they satisfy them with material ministries or capture them with the devious bait of glitter and ease. It is the clarion challenge of the Strait Gate that awakens, arrests, and apprehends. Men lives by narrowing.

Narrowness is the way to power. The narrowness of bigotry strangles. Narrowness for service makes for efficiency. The man who chooses, narrows his interests, energies, and life to a given end. A narrower Church may mean a smaller Church, though experience rather proves the reverse, but it will be a Church of the Holy Presence, skilled in the ministry of consolation, powerful in the building of character, and mighty in the power of the Spirit for the Salvation of those for whom Christ died.

Twenty-fifth Sunday after Trinity

The Reigning Lamb
Revelation 5

The Lamb redeems, and the Lamb reigns. None but the Lamb can have universal dominion. All other thrones divide. The Lamb reconciles. Power strengthens barriers; Love breaks them down. Nationalism is the prolific breeder of war. Class interest engenders strife. Love has no frontiers. Lions are mighty to crush. Lambs can do nothing but give and bleed. Love is universal. Love gives all, to all, for all. Thrones are prepared for Love. That was John's great discovery in the Kingdom of Heaven, and it gave him the surprise of his life. 'After these things I saw, and behold, a great number, which no man could number, out of every nation and of all tribes and people and tongues, standing before the Lamb, arrayed in white robes, and palms in their hands.' His Throne takes precedence over all other thrones, and His Kingdom supersedes all nationalities. In Him there is neither Jew nor Greek. In the kingdoms of this world a sword reigns; upon the Throne of God is a Bleeding Lamb. The way to the Throne goes by the way of a Cross. This was true for our Lord. It is also true for His followers; and it is certainly true in the life of nations. The Throne of God must be supreme, and the Lamb must reign if peace is to prevail.

The third book mentioned is, *The Call to Christian Perfection*, and it was published in 1943, 1944, 1950, and it was published again in 2013. This writer has the one published in 1950 ranging from 'The Accent of Wesley's Teaching,' to 'The Prayer for Christian Perfection.' Chadwick never saw the book in print but he would have rejoiced to see Wesley's teaching published. It was his conviction from the age of twenty-two when he was lay Pastor at Stacksteads to his death in 1932, that this great evangel was the theme of John Wesley's teaching and he preached it all his life. Wesley's teaching was all of a piece and he never invented any new doctrine. *The Call to Christian Perfection* Wesley found in the Old and New Testament and he never varied from this theme.

> John Wesley had no doctrinal eccentricities and to the end he was a doctrinal clergymen of the Church of England. He made no new discovery, he produced no new theory and invented no new dogma. The peculiarity of his teaching lay in its accent. It produced the old truth with a living voice, spoken with a living voice and heard in England with a new and living accent. Academic truth kills but living truth saves and sanctifies and Wesley only speaks of what he has found in the Bible. The Methodist doctrines of conversion, assurance, and full salvation, can be traced to marked crises in his own experience of the saving grace of God. The Methodist peculiarities of fellowship, testimony, and aggression, were all first exemplified in the religious life of the first Methodist. He is the explanation of every essential peculiar of the great Methodist movement. He anticipated the developments of two hundred years, and every movement is discovered to be but a return to first principles.[62]

The first distinctive note of his creed was the universality of the gospel of Christ. Christ had died for all and the gates of the eternal kingdom were flung wide for all; the feast of the Father's house were spread for all. There was no limitation, exemption or preference. He had heard the voice of God commanding him to go forth and calling all men and women to repent and be saved. The secret of his confidence was his own experience of the grace of God. From the moment he himself was accepted, he was debtor to all, and despaired of none. It is difficult for

---

62 Samuel Chadwick, *The Call to Christian Perfection,* 1950, pp.5, 6.

us to realise the startling novelty of such teaching in Wesley's day. To us it is a commonplace but to the eighteenth century it was a revelation. The England to which the great revival came was wrapped in dense darkness. Rationalism had quenched the altar fire and brutality had taken possession of the people. If the Established Church was asleep in the dark, the Dissenting were as truly asleep in the light. But religion was a thing apart, and its followers were elect and separate from the common faith of men. Calvinism was the dominant creed and Calvinism in its baldest form means monopoly, privilege and caste. John Wesley fought Calvinism with all his might and he preached everywhere the gospel of universal love. It offered salvation for all on equal terms. It was for the boy in the stable, as much as for the heir in the palace; for the man at the plough as truly as for the man in the pulpit; for the sinner in the gutter, as well as for the saint in the curtained pew. Pious people were scandalised that the vulgar and reprobate should be welcomed to the privileges of the Father's house.

Wesley was the first great evangelist in this country to whom was given the privilege of preaching through the length and breadth of the land this glorious gospel in which there is no restriction, limitation or reserve. What John Wesley preached, his brother, Charles Wesley, sang. The Methodist Hymn-book is the manual of Methodist experience. The hymn everywhere strike the note of universality.

Come, sinners, to the gospel feast
Let every soul be Jesu's guest
You need not one be left behind
For God hath bidden all mankind.

Sent by my Lord, on you I call
The invitation is to all
Come, all the world; come, sinner, thou
All things in Christ are ready now.

Charles Wesley

There are twenty four verses to this hymn and all twenty-four strike the note – Jesus Christ died for all. There is no possibility of mistaking the invitation, and the same note runs through all their songs. They went everywhere, saying to every man and woman:

> O let me commend my Saviour to you.

John Wesley did not give himself to academic discussion but by preaching of the Word, and by his persistent testimony he gave the death-blow to the doctrine which limited the possibility of salvation to the favoured few.

Not less conspicuous than the doctrine of universalism was Wesley's teaching of assurance. This was a prominent feature of Wesley's own experience.

> 'In the evening (May 24, 1738), I went very unwillingly to a Society in Aldersgate Street, where one was reading Luther's preface to the Epistle to the Romans. About a quarter before nine, while he was describing the change which God works in the heart, through faith in Christ, I felt my heart strangely warmed. I felt I did trust in Christ, Christ alone, for salvation; and an assurance was given me that He had taken away my sins, even mine, and saved me from the law of sin and death.' An assurance was given him, and to that assurance he testified openly on the spot. He lived in the enjoyment of an assured acceptance, and preached its privilege to all who would trust in Christ, Christ alone, for salvation.... The convert were gathered into Society Classes, where all spoke frankly of the experience of God in the soul. No wonder they sang! They were children of God and heirs of heaven. Love feasts became great rallying centres, where men and women testified of the wonderful works of God. All distinctions of rank, wealth, and culture disappeared. All were one in Christ and the Methodist people became a brotherhood, a radiant family of God. The witness of the Spirit is now conceded to be the privilege of sonship, but it was the Wesleys who brought it to the people. Wherever Methodists gathered it was preached and sung.[63]

How he defined Christian Perfection was John Wesley's crowning ambition. He preached it, expounded it, defended it, and insisted upon it continually. It laid him open to scurrilous attack and scandalous

---

63 Samuel Chadwick, *The Call to Christian Perfection*, pp.9-11.

misrepresentation but he never wavered. Its statement was the greatest work of his life, and its literature his unique contribution to the doctrines of the Church. He escaped many common perils common to definitions by confining himself to scriptural expressions. In 1769 he avowed that Christian holiness was as Christ taught it, and writing to a lady not known, he averred:

> And with regard to perfection. Have not they that hold it the same right to be angry with you for denying it as you with them for affirming it? But what is it you are angry at? What is it you object to? Let us understand the question before we dispute about it. By Christian Perfection I mean; (1) loving God with our heart. Do you object to this? I mean (2) a heart and life all devoted to God. Do you desire less? I mean (3) regaining the whole image of God. What objection to this? I mean (4) having all the mind that was in Christ. Is this going too far? I mean (5) walking uniformly as Christ walked. And this surely no Christian will object to. If any one means anything more or anything less else by perfection, I have no concern with it.[64]

Wesley wrote in 1766 a treatise entitled, *A Plain Account of Christian Perfection*, which to this day is unsurpassed, as a statement and defence of the doctrine. It is a great testimony to his sanity, caution and scriptural fidelity that, after two hundred and fifty years of Christian progress, nothing has been added nor any defect discovered in his teaching upon the subject. His steady, clear light is still the best guide to the Canaan of perfect love. In this, as in everything else, he was a man of action. He inquired of all his preachers, regularly, whether they had received the gift of perfect love. If their testimony was not very clear, the question was followed by another: 'Are they groaning after it? ' Everywhere he inquired if believers were living in the enjoyment of entire sanctification. Nothing less was sufficient. Even new converts were urged to seek full salvation, the deliverance from the presence of inbred sin. He observed that where the blessing was neglected the cause languished. The entire sanctification of believers was followed by the conversion of the ungodly.

---

64 John Wesley, *The Letters of the Rev. John Wesley*, Vol. 5, p.141.

On this subject the Methodist Hymn Book is the best guide to this doctrine. Chadwick was using the Methodist Hymn Book of 1932 and between now and then that book has gone through two editions and in each edition the number of hymns has decreased. Between 1933 and 1997 the version of hymns has decreased and what we should be looking at is the book published in London in June 1904. The place to look is 'For Believers Seeking Full Redemption,' and there is plenty of those. They throb with the holiest aspirations of the soul, and pulsate with the indwelling life of God. As Paul's prayers are the best expositions of his theology, so these Methodist hymns are the best exponents of the Methodist doctrine. Here is one doctrine that believers' are seeking for.

O come and dwell in me
Spirit of power within
And bring the glorious liberty
From sorrow, fear and sin.

The seed of sin's disease
Spirit of health remove
Spirit of finished holiness
Spirit of perfect love.

The original offence
Out of my soul erase
Enter Thyself, and drive it hence
And take up all the place.

538 The Methodist Hymn Book, 1904

This blessing was declared to be the gift of God and wrought in the soul by the sanctifying spirit of truth. It is preceded by conviction and received through faith.

That I Thy mercy may proclaim
That all mankind Thy truth may see
Hallow Thy great and glorious name
And perfect holiness in me.
O that I now from sin released
Thy word may to the utmost prove
Enter into the promised rest

The Canaan of Thy perfect love.
548 The Methodist Hymn Book, 1904

This is the scriptural holiness that John Wesley preached and Methodism was raised up to spread through the land. This is the gospel that he preached; a gospel of present, free, universal salvation; a gospel of complete deliverance from all outward and inward sin, a gospel of grace so perfect that the whole life is maintained in the will of God.

Saviour to Thee my soul looks up
My present Saviour Thou
In all the confidence of hope
I claim the blessing now.
'Tis done, Thou dost this moment save
With full salvation bless
Redemption through Thy blood I have
And spotless love and peace.
560 The Methodist Hymn Book, 1904

John Wesley found England in the grip of the doctrines of election and predestination. Calvinism did reverent homage to the sovereignty of God, and it produced saints of mighty power, but it emphasized God to the neglect of man. Its sovereignty became arbitrary, meretricious, and almost capricious, until it was a caricature of the God and Father of Jesus Christ. The Calvinism of ecclesiasticism had a corresponding Calvinism in secular and national life. The elect were few, the rest were reprobate. Election was not according to merit, but by birth and favour. The elect possessed all things. They had all the land, all the wealth, all the votes, all the learning, and everything else worth having in the nation. A democratic gospel changed all that. The Evangelical Revival carried everywhere a gospel of equality before God. The revival saved the land from revolution. The man in the street got the Methodist conception of Christianity with the result that national life has been remodelled on that of Methodist doctrine. There are thousands in the churches who have not so much as heard of perfect love as a present possession. The gospel which made the democracy is the only gospel by which the democracy can be saved. There Methodism will find her conquest or her grave.

Chapter two is called 'The Doctrine of Christian Perfection,' and Wesley sets out a restatement. His doctrine of the new birth was incomplete and truth needs to be reborn for the new age. New problems call for new developments and Wesley was one that looked for new ways of thinking.

> His teaching was experimental and he refused to be entangled in philosophical speculations. He never shirked a practical problem but he could only deal with those of his own age. Principles are eternal and universal but rules are determined by times and circumstances. His anxiety to avoid all suspicion of preaching 'a sinless perfection' led him to reckon in the category of sins some infirmities and limitations which are entirely destitute of moral character. It is never satisfactory to have a problem dismissed with a gesture, as when he answers the question, 'Is it sinless?' with the remark, 'It is not worth while to contend for a term; it is salvation from sin.' The contention is for clearness of thought, intelligence of faith, and instruction in the implications of experience. We have to plead guilty to the charge that we have not been faithful stewards of this 'depositum' of grace. There is with one consent a culpable silence on the subject. For sixteen years I heard candidates for ordination asked if they ever preached specifically and definitely on the subject of Holiness as an experience, and the answer was always the same. All their preaching was on Holiness, but they had not specifically expounded or urged the experience.[65]

The Bible is every man's best guide but teaching is necessary, otherwise God would not have included it among His gifts to the Church. Wesley is often commended for his sagacity in defining the doctrine in terms of Scriptures, and for the purposes of controversy it was proof of his wisdom. For instruction in the faith something more is needed than to be told that: 'Pure love reigning in the heart is the whole of Christian Perfection.' No words could set before the mind a higher ideal, a simpler principle, or a greater incentive. Faith needs to be instructed, and the heart must be able to give reasons for its experience and hope. Christian teachers must translate their theology into speech of the twenty-first century. Revival is more important than re-statement. Testimony to the possession of the blessing is

[65] Samuel Chadwick, *The Call to Christian Perfection*, pp.21, 22.

exceedingly rare. To fathers there was given a witness of the Spirit to be a definite gift as distinct as that borne to adoption. God's ambassadors are witnesses as well as messengers. In how many pulpits is it heard throughout the year? Failure in fellowship has its roots far deeper than the changes in social life. What about the theological training of the ministry? Is the doctrine expounded with clearness and the experience urged upon those who are to be future leaders in the Church? Is there not occasion to ask whether the doctrine is any longer believed and taught by those who possess the blessing?

Chapter five of this book is entitled, 'Christian Perfection as Interpreted by John Wesley.' His theology was experimental and his statements were formulated from experience. His life was lived in a perpetual hurricane of controversy and incessant activity. He was an evangelist first and only incidentally a philosopher and a theologian. His system of Church government is embodied in a legal document, designed to secure the property of his people and the fellowship of his spiritual children. His principles were well and truly laid, and he had learned to distinguish between principles and opinion, things eternal and unchanging, and those which are temporary and provisional. For half a century he was stating, restating and defending the doctrine of scriptural holiness. He examined thousands who professed to have entered into the experience. He himself testifies to its possession, and for years contended that the Methodist people were raised up to be its exponents, and to spread it through the land.

He preached it as an immediate, instantaneous, assured work of grace through faith. By it the believer is delivered from inbred sin. Then John Wesley quotes from his, A *Plain Account of Christian Perfection.*

> It may be observed, this sermon was composed the first of all my writings which have been published. This was the view of religion I had then, which even then I scrupled not to term *perfection*. This is the view I have of it now, without any material addition or diminution. And what is there here, which any man of understanding, who believes the Bible, can object to? What can he deny, without flatly contradicting the

> Scriptures? What retrench, without taking from the word of God?[66].... These are the very words wherein I largely declared, for the first time, my sentiments of Christian perfection. And is it not easy to see, (1) That this is the very point at which I aimed all along.... (2) That this is the same doctrine which I believed and teach at this day; not adding one point, either to the inward or outward holiness which I maintained eight and thirty years ago. And it is the same degree which, by the grace of God, I have continued to teach from that time till now.[67]

This is plain, sound, scriptural experience and these the seals to his preaching and the crown of his rejoicing. Wesley insisted on all his preachers expounding and explicitly urging this doctrine of full salvation. Writing to Adam Clarke on November 26, 1790, just three months before he died, on this doctrine, he says: 'If we can prove that any of our local preachers or leaders, either directly or indirectly speak against it, let him be a local preacher or leader no longer. I doubt whether he should continue in society. Because he that could speak thus in our society cannot be an honest man.'[68]

John Wesley was bitterly assailed for his teaching on Christian perfection. It cost him some of his most valued friends and exposed him to all kinds of calumny and misrepresentation. His doctrine was attacked from opposite sides. Some objected that he placed the standard too high. The Calvinists charged him with making void the gospel of faith, because he insisted upon inward cleansing from all sin and a life in which the love of God reigns supreme. He demanded nothing less than obedience to all the commandments of God. This is Wesley's standard of perfection. To this day the attack is maintained by the representatives of thc Calvinistic persuasion. Eradication of inward sin is held to be impossible in this life. Subjugation is all we may hope for. Perfectionism is assailed as deadly heresy. The old questions of Wesley's reappear in modern form. Does salvation from sin mean that Christians live without sin, what need will the sanctified have of the atoning blood? To make the death of Christ an occasion of

---

[66] John Wesley, '*A Plain Account of Christian Perfection*', Vol. 11, p.369.
[67] John Wesley, '*A Plain Account of Christian Perfection*', Vol. 11, p.373.
[68] John Wesley, *The Letters of John Wesley*, Vol. 8, p.249.

release from perfect obedience comes very near to making the Cross the minister of sin.

Opposition comes also from the other extreme. While some charge him with putting the standard too high, others contend he puts it too low, because he says that no man is able to perform the service which the Adamic law requires. On this subject there is certainly some ambiguity in Wesley's teaching. He declines to call Christian perfection sinless and yet he insists that it is salvation from all sin. There is need for elucidation and co-ordination of his teaching. The explanation will probably be found in an exaggerated view of Adam's original perfection, and, if one dare say it, a somewhat lax and popular use of the word 'sin.' Whatever the explanation, no man familiar with Wesley's teaching will charge him with making void the law. He never spoke of the law as having passed away, in any sense, but as ceremonial ordinance and a condition of justification. Salvation is by faith and not by the works of the law, but the perfect law remains in force as the standard of life and obedience. The law is immutable, universal, and eternal, a transcript of the divine nature. The law of love is not new. It is no lowering of the standard. It is the fulfilling of the law. Grace does not release from obedience; it empowers it.

Christ Jesus came into the world to save sinners. The seat of sin is in the soul. Christian perfection is salvation from sin. A higher meaning than this it cannot have; a lower meaning it must not have. Sin defaced God's image in man, and turned his love to enmity; Jesus restores the image and turns enmity to love. By Him provision is made that the righteousness of the law might be fulfilled in us. The law is not a system of statutes to be mechanically observed, but a principle of love possible alike to angels and men; love filling the heart and reigning in the life of all those who are God-minded. The same commandment is laid upon all, and the same privilege of grace is open to all.

Chapter six is entitled, *Christian Perfection in Relation to Sins and Mistakes.* Chadwick points to St. John's teaching concerning sin and that settles it for all time. Chapter three of his First Epistle emphatically declares:

1. That sin is lawlessness.
2. Jesus Christ was manifested to take away sins.
3. Whosoever is begotten of God, and abides in Him, does not commit sin.
4. The difference between the children of God and the children of the devil is that the one sins and the other does not.

Nothing can be plainer than this. Every man born of God quits sin. If a man sins, he is not a child of God but a child of Satan.

Spiritual kinship is not of blood but of spirit. Though men belong by right to God they may be by choice the possession of the devil. We are the work of God's hands and the people of His pasture. We may have been born in sin and shapen in iniquity, but for all that we belong to God, not Satan. Original sin is counterbalanced by original grace. No soul belongs to Satan either by any vestige or right or by the law of necessity. The sonship of the covenant avails only until moral responsibility is attained. The Timothys need to be born again as truly as the Ishmaels. Spiritual parentage is by adoption. There can be no adoption without consent. In the spiritual realm every man chooses his one Father. On the other hand, the first chapter of John says: 'If we say that we have no sin, we deceive ourselves, and the truth is not in us' (1 John 1:8). These passages present a real difficulty. They seem to be absolutely contradictory, that if one be true the other must be false; and it is between these two statements we find the most contention. Some contend for the absolute deliverance of the soul from sin, and others for the inevitable continuance of sin in the soul.

The explanation will be found in a complete study of John's treatment of the doctrine of sin. He defines it as lawlessness. Sin is not an act but an attitude. Man is not so much a sinner because he is a transgressor, as he is a transgressor because he is a sinner. Its seat is neither in the body nor in the mind; it is the heart. In chapter one he exposes three false views of sin. If we deny the reality of sin under cloak of fellowship with God, we lie and do not live out the truth (1:6). If we deny our responsibility for sin, we deceive ourselves and the truth is not in us (1:8). If we deny the fact of sin and say we have not sinned, we make

> God a liar and His Word is not in us (1:10). None of these passages teach that sin must always be in us, or that we must inevitably keep on sinning. He pardons and cleanses those who confess their sin, and the blood of His Son cleanses from all sin those who walk in the light. This does not mean that the Christian can never again fall away into sin. All scripture – John's writings included – warns us that the child of God can fall into sin. He has been made partaker of the divine nature and the bent of his nature is one with God's.[69]

Christian perfection has been regarded as claiming not only deliverance from sin, but from all error, limitation and defect. Christian perfection is not infallibility. A clean heart does not imply a perfect head. As long as we are in this world there will be unavoidably errors and imperfection of judgement. Such imperfections are utterly destitute of moral character and they need no repentance. Sanctification reduces liability to error to a minimum, but it does not guarantee infallibility; and while we have an adversary so subtle and a nature so liable to sin, we shall never rise above the need to pray, 'Forgive us our trespasses.' The vision of a pure heart is always discovering new demands of grace and a new sensibility of sin. It is better to live a sinless life than to say we never sin.

Samuel Chadwick goes on in his teaching and calls chapter nine, *Do the Scriptures Teach a Second Blessing?* Proof by isolated texts can be made to prove anything. Truths flows through a thousand channels and doctrine must gather up all phases in its ultimate statement. For this reason it is not enough to buttress a statement by texts; the statement must be the final issue of all the texts. The Second Blessing is not in a text; it is in the whole Bible. Because the man who has found it sees it everywhere, it is difficult for him to prove it anywhere. There is an unction of the Holy One by which the sanctified are led into the truth. The pure in heart see and love made perfect sanctifies all life and perfects the knowledge of divine things. Hereby we know, and know that we know, if we keeps His commandments.

---

[69] Samuel Chadwick, *Christian Perfection in Relation to Sins and Mistakes*, pp.55, 56.

People often ask why a doctrine so important is not more explicitly stated and commanded in the Bible. The same question applies to all doctrines within the Kingdom. The command to repent and believe, the necessity of forgiveness and regeneration, are definite and explicit enough, because these are concerned with them that are without. When once the boundary is passed, truth has to be discovered. Jesus commanded His disciples to tell no man He was the Christ. The Spirit leads each into the possession of truth, that can only be received by the experiment of personal faith. Those who are keen to know that they may possess will find it fully set forth in the Scriptures. There is no other guide nor any other authority. The Bible is its own interpreter and they that will to know that they may do, will not seek in vain.

> That the Scriptures require us to be holy, no one denies. Without holiness no man or woman can ever enter heaven. He came to save from sin. Christ redeems, that He may cleanse and restore. Scripture and experience affirm it. The Christians at Corinth were sanctified and yet carnal (1:2; 3:1-3). They were exhorted to cleanse themselves 'from all defilement of the flesh and spirit, perfecting holiness in the fear of God' (2 Cor. 7:1). The Galatians had received the spirit of adoption, and to them Paul said, 'The flesh lusteth against the Spirit, and the Spirit against the flesh' (Gal. 5:17). The New Testament saints were true believers, and carnality remained in them. Thus people already in a state of grace are urged to an experience of cleansing and fullness. This cleansing is by faith. It is a definite act with a definite aim. The apostle desired to come again to the believers at Thessalonica, that he might 'perfect that which was lacking in their faith,' and the desire was expressed in the prayer: 'And the God of peace Himself sanctify you wholly; and may your spirit and soul and body be preserved entire, without blame, at the coming of our Lord Jesus Christ. Faithful is He that calleth you, who will also do it.'[70]

Chadwick then deals with a major problem and he calls this, *Difficulties About Christian Perfection.* Perhaps it will be best to begin with the confession. This is the experience of everybody who hopes to grow into the blessing. It never comes by growth, either unurged or forced. The evil grows with the good until the evil is purged out. Surely

---

[70] Samuel Chadwick, *Do the Scriptures Teach a Second Blessing?*, pp.79, 80.

it cannot be consistent with the gospel of a Saviour who is able to save to the uttermost, that we should be striving and for ever failing. His purpose is that we should be saved with a present, free, and full salvation, and His grace is equal to His purpose. Salvation is not of works, but of grace through faith. The work is not begun in grace and perfected in works. It is the gift of God. Chadwick was well versed in Professor Drummond's, *Natural Law in the Spiritual World*, and notes that evolution breaks down, both in Nature and in Grace. There are creative epochs which lift life into a new plane, implant a new quality, and impart a new power. The experience of the perfecting of grace is a crisis and an epoch. Tens of thousands have testified to the experience, and not one of them ever achieved it by endeavour. Without exception they received it as a gift of grace through faith.

The blood that cleanses from all sin purges out of the heart all pride. Lowliness and meekness come of the vision by which the pure in heart see God. The blessing of full salvation saves from pride and envy and all false estimates of worth and virtue. It is stranger still to imagine that holiness makes us hard and unsympathetic toward sinful people. A heart of compassion is the fruit of holiness. Holiness brings the soul into fellowship with the redeeming Son of God. When believers rejoice in its possession, sinners are awakened and saved. Four months before he died, John Wesley wrote a letter to Robert Carr Brackenbury in which he said: 'I am glad Brother Dieuside has more light with regard to full sanctification. This doctrine is the grand depositum which God has lodged with the people called Methodists; and for the sake of propagating this chiefly He appeared to have raised us up.'[71]

Chadwick then raises the question of whether perfection is the cause of much confusion among those to whom he is writing.

> The real difficulty seems to be in the term 'perfection.' I have been explaining it for thirty years, and failure to understand the use of the term in two different senses is amazing. Take Philippians 3. The apostle disavows perfection in verse 12, and affirms it in verse 15. The two cannot mean the same in such contradictory statements. The first

---

[71] John Wesley, *The Letters of John Wesley*, Vol. 8, p.238.

> obviously refers to a future perfecting in the glory of the resurrection; the other is a present experience. In the present he is perfect, but not perfected. There is no finality in the perfection of grace, but in the resurrection grace will be perfected in the consummation of redemption. The great prayer for perfection in Hebrews 13:20, 21, is the best statement of both the doctrine and the experience. It is being made perfect in every good thing to do His will, and if grace cannot do this it is useless to talk of an uttermost salvation.[72]

Samuel Chadwick rounds off his book by the chapter, *The Prayer For Christian Perfection.* He starts off with a prayer from the Bible:
'Now the God of peace, which brought again from the dead our Lord Jesus, that great shepherd of the sheep, through the blood of the everlasting covenant, make you perfect in every good work, working in us that which is well-pleasing in his sight, through Jesus Christ, to whom be the glory for ever and ever. Amen' (Heb. 13:20, 21).

It is not for any man or woman to say that he or she is perfect. The doctrine is scriptural and the defence of it sound, but the profession of the experience in terms of perfection is not to be commended. It may be true but it is not expedient. Other terms have been used but they are less expressive than those of scripture. Perfect love is scriptural and interpretative. Full salvation is comprehensive and less definite, and that is true also of the terms which set forth the fullness of the Spirit.

Perfection belongs to the language of prayer. Christian truth finds sublimest expression in prayer. There are no expositions of faith like those in the inspired prayer of holy Scriptures. Language finds its wings in the prayer life of the soul. Prayer is an exercise that calls for every faculty of man's nature. There are people who are naturally slow of speech who were wonderfully gifted in prayer. Prayer reviews life and motive in the light of His countenance. There is always something to correct, something to improve, something to claim. Prayer cannot ask too much. Christian perfection is surrender to, acceptance of, and efficiency in, all the will of God. It is not the attainment of some

---

[72] Samuel Chadwick, *Difficulties About Christian Perfection*, pp.101, 102.

mystical ecstasy, or the achievement of some heroic sacrifice, but just doing the will of God out of a pure heart.

God has given guaranties of His ability and good faith. It is not a question of man's will and ability, but of God's purpose and power. Chadwick believes in holiness because he believes in the holiness of God. Faith affirms His ability to do. His very nature demands it for He is the God of peace. He makes peace, He gives peace, ever perfect peace. There are no antagonisms He cannot reconcile, no dislocations He cannot adjust, no discords He cannot harmonize, no faults He cannot remedy, no disease He cannot heal, no lack He cannot supply. He is the God of peace, and peace is the perfect relation of every part to every other part, and of all the parts to the whole.

He has proved His power. He brought again from the dead our Lord Jesus. The resurrection of our Lord from the dead is not mentioned elsewhere in the letter to the Hebrews, and it is cited here as a guarantee of God's power to make His people perfect. The resurrection of our Lord Jesus is the New Testament standard of measurement for the power of God. It is the big thing by which all other things are measured.

He has provided a Great Saviour. The Risen Lord is the 'Great Shepherd.' The Shepherd is everything to His flock. He protects and provides, leads and loves, heals and helps, corrects and controls. The Lamb of God has become the Shepherd of His people, and He shepherds them that they neither hunger nor thirst, for He leads them by still waters and living fountains. Chadwick goes on to say that he believes in holiness because he believes in the Great Shepherd.

> God has put it in the covenant. Through the blood of the everlasting covenant the prayer for perfection is made. God has sworn by an oath. It is His will we should be made perfect in every good thing to do His will. His only begotten Son is surety for His word. He has undertaken it on covenant terms. It is a wonderful covenant, for in it God pledges Himself and undertakes for us. I love the covenant relationship. The blood of the cross is the security for our perfecting. I believe in Holiness because I believe in the covenant through the blood of the cross. That is

the Christian Perfection set forth in the great prayer which closes the epistle on the Perfect Son, the Perfect Saviour, and the Perfect Salvation. How can I but believe that such a Saviour is able to save to the uttermost, and make me perfect in every good thing to do His will?[73]

Jesus, the First and Last
On Thee my soul is cast
Thou didst Thy work begin
By blotting out my sin
Thou wilt the root remove
And perfect me in love.
Yet when the work is done
The work is but begun
Partaker of Thy grace
I long to see Thy face
The first I prove below
The last I die to know.

Charles Wesley (The Poetical Works, 13:221)

[73] Samuel Chadwick, *The Prayer for Christian Perfection*, pp.109, 110.

Selected Bibliography

K.F. Bowden, *Samuel Chadwick and Stacksteads*, Stackststeads, 1982.

Samuel Chadwick, *Humanity And God*, Hodder and Stoughton, London, 1903.

The Path of Prayer, Hodder and Stoughton, 1931.

The Way to Pentecost, Hodder and Stoughton, 1932.

The Gospel Of The Cross, Epworth Press, 1934.

The Way Of The Cross, Hodder And Stoughton, n.d. London.

The Call to Christian Perfection, Beacon Hill Press, Kansas City, 1943.

God Listens: To The Crying Heart in The Secret Places, Good News Publishers, Illinois, 1973.

James M. Gordon, *Evangelical Spirituality: From The Wesleys To John Stott,* SPCK, London, 1991.

D.W. Lambert, *25 Sunday Mornings with Samuel Chadwick,* Epworth Press, London, 1951.

25 Sunday Evenings with Samuel Chadwick, Epworth Press, 1954.

The Testament of Samuel Chadwick 1860-1932, Epworth Press, London, 1957.

Through the Year with Samuel Chadwick, Epworth Press, London, 1960.

David H. Howarth, *How Great A Flame,* Cliff College, 1983.

A. Skevington Wood, *Let Us Go On*, Moorleys, Ilkeston, 1985.

Books by Revd Dr Herbert Boyd McGonigle

William Cooke on Entire Sanctification, Beacon Hill Press, Kansas City, Missouri, 1978.

The Arminianism of John Wesley, Moorleys Print & Publishing, Ilkeston, Derbyshire, 1988.

John Wesley and the Moravians, Moorleys Print & Publishing, Ilkeston, Derbyshire, 1995.

John Wesley's Doctrine of Prevenient Grace, Moorleys Print & Publishing, Ilkeston, Derbyshire, 1995.

Scriptural Holiness: The Wesleyan Distinctive, Moorleys Print & Publishing, Ilkeston, Derbyshire, 1995.

Sufficient Saving Grace: John Wesley's Evangelical Arminianism, 350 pages, Paternoster Publishing, Carlisle, Cumbria, 2001.

To God Be The Glory: The Killadeas Convention 1952-2002, Moorleys Print & Publishing, Ilkeston, Derbyshire, 2002.

John Wesley's Arminian Theology: An Introduction, Moorleys Print & Publishing, Ilkeston, Derbyshire, 2005.

A Burning and a Shining Light: The Life and Ministry of William Bramwell, Moorleys Print & Publishing, Ilkeston, Derbyshire, 2009.

Christianity or Deism? John Wesley's Response to John Taylor's Denial of the Doctrine of Original Sin, Moorleys Print & Publishing, Ilkeston, Derbyshire, 2012.

John Wesley: Exemplar of the Catholic Spirit, Moorleys Print & Publishing, Ilkeston, Derbyshire, 2014.

Charles Wesley: For All, For All My Saviour Died, Moorleys Print & Publishing, Ilkeston, Derbyshire, 2014.

John Wesley: The Death of Christ, Moorleys Print & Publishing, Ilkeston, Derbyshire, 2014.

Epworth: The Cradle of Methodism, Moorleys Print & Publishing, Ilkeston, Derbyshire, 2014.

John Wesley: Doctrine of Final Judgement, Moorleys Print & Publishing, Ilkeston, Derbyshire, 2015.

Thomas Walsh: Saint and Scholar, Moorleys Print & Publishing, Ilkeston, Derbyshire, 2015.

Our Story: Autobiographical thoughts from the pen of Revd. Dr. Herbert B. McGonigle, Nazarene Theological College Archives, Manchester, 2015.

Dr. Adam Clarke: Methodist Preacher and Scholar, Moorleys Print & Publishing, Ilkeston, Derbyshire, 2015.

Gideon Ouseley: Methodist Preacher and Biblical Scholar, Moorleys Print & Publishing, Ilkeston, Derbyshire, 2015.

Thomas Cook: Evangelist and Saint, Moorleys Print & Publishing, Ilkeston, Derbyshire, 2016.

The Methodist Pentecost, 1758-1763, Moorleys Print & Publishing, Ilkeston, Derbyshire, 2016.

John Fletcher, Methodist Saint and Scholar, Moorleys Print & Publishing, Ilkeston, Derbyshire, 2016.

An Appreciation of Revd. Dr. John Henry Jowett's Heaven's Hallelujah, Moorleys Print & Publishing, Ilkeston, Derbyshire, 2016.

General William Booth, Moorleys Print & Publishing, Ilkeston, Derbyshire, 2016.

John Wesley on The Great Salvation, Moorleys Bookshop, Ilkeston, Derbyshire, 2017.